LESSER KNOWN BIBLE CHARACTERS

Blessings,
Carolyn H. Roth

LESSER KNOWN BIBLE CHARACTERS

USING THEIR RELATIONSHIPS TO RESTORE OURS

DR. CAROLYN A. ROTH

TATE PUBLISHING
AND ENTERPRISES, LLC

Published by Tate Publishing & Enterprises, LLC
127 E. Trade Center Terrace | Mustang, Oklahoma 73064 USA
1.888.361.9473 | www.tatepublishing.com

Tate Publishing is committed to excellence in the publishing industry. The company reflects the philosophy established by the founders, based on Psalm 68:11,
"The Lord gave the word and great was the company of those who published it."

Book design copyright © 2015 by Tate Publishing, LLC. All rights reserved.
Cover design by Norlan Balazo
Interior design by Jake Muelle

Published in the United States of America

ISBN: 978-1-68142-934-2
1. Religion / Biblical Studies / Exegesis & Hermeneutics
2. Religion / Biblical Meditations / General
15.07.16

To my husband, Bruce Roth

ACKNOWLEDGMENTS

Thank you to:

- Karen Hatzigeorgiou at Christian Image Source (www.christianimagesource.com) for making available the photographs and illustrations in this book.
- Tate Publishing and Enterprises, LLC for publishing my second Christian book.

CONTENTS

PREFACE

As you read through the Bible, you discover hundreds of individuals who were mentioned only once or twice; i.e., Hirah, Ish-Bosheth, Tattenai. They appeared, only to promptly disappear in the next couple of verses or chapter. Generally, their personalities were poorly developed, their actions rarely explained. Like me, you may have wondered why God gave them space in the holy scriptures. Surely, a more important character, action, or truth could have been put in the limited Bible space?

The apostle Paul answered our question, "Why are they even there?" He wrote that all scripture is valuable for teaching, rebuking, correcting, and training in righteousness. God breathed lesser known characters into the Bible to give us information we need to fulfill the work God planned for us here on earth. That means we are to learn from the lives and behaviors of these lesser known Bible characters. Their actions—the ones consistent with God's commands and those outside God's guidelines—are object lessons for our lives.

As I read and reread Bible stories of lesser known characters, I saw that they didn't act in isolation. None was a hermit or recluse. None acted independently from other individuals in their environment. All were in one or more relationship, and these relationships influenced their behavior. From these observations, I concluded that the optimal way to study lesser known Bible characters was to look at their relational behavior.

Behavior has meaning. Some meanings are obvious while others are obscure. Some behavior is admirable because it reflects God's morality and justice. Other behavior is appalling and, yes, even disgusting to us. As a nurse-psychologist, few activities are more exciting than investigating causes and meanings of human behavior. What better place to learn from human behavior than holy scripture.

When investigating lesser-known Bible characters, I used both study and archeology Bibles, *The Works of Josephus* translated by William Whiston, Jewish midrash literature, and books on cultural and societal norms of ancient peoples. The *African Bible Commentary (2006)*, edited by Tobunboh Adeyemo, was particularly insightful. Some current African cultures and beliefs parallel those of Old Testament cultures. Be sure to check out the reference list at the end of the book.

Chapter 1

Husband and Wives

After God created and formed a relationship with Adam, God created a wife for him. This creation sequence demonstrated that the most important relationship in an individual's life is with God, followed by the husband-wife—or marriage—relationship. God created Eve to be Adam's helpmeet. She assisted Adam to tend the beautiful Garden of Eden, made his life more pleasant, and completed him. Interestingly, the archaic meaning of the word *help* is "to rescue." Eve rescued Adam from a loneliness that he wasn't aware of.

In marriage, a husband and wife are one flesh. A husband's body doesn't belong to himself alone, but to his wife. Likewise, a wife's body doesn't belong to herself alone, but to her husband. Husbands and wives aren't to deprive themselves of sexual fulfillment, unless by mutual consent for a time of fasting and prayer. Then, they should come together again. Prolonged abstinence from the marriage partner can lead to sexual immorality.

The apostle Paul directed husbands to love their wives as Christ loves the church. The way Christ loves the church is with overwhelming, never-ending love. In his love for the church, Christ models forgiveness, gentleness, goodness, humility, and every positive attribute imaginable. Also, St. Paul directed men to love their wives as they love their own bodies; however, Christ demonstrated that he loves the church more than he loved his own body. He died for the church.

As the church submits to Christ, wives submit to husbands. Although Paul wrote in Greek, the Hebrew word for submit is more descriptive than the Greek word. In Hebrew, *submit* is derived from *châzaq*, which means to seize or fasten upon, take courage from, and help (Strong, 2010).

When Paul encouraged wives to submit to their husbands, he meant for wives to hold onto them and take courage from their presence. At the same time, a wife has to help her husband.

Christ told his disciples that after he left God would send the Holy Spirit to them (John 14:26). Although some Bibles name the Holy Spirit the Comforter (KJV) and the Counselor (NIV), both the English Standard Version Study Bible (ESV) and New American Standard Bible (NASB) identified the Holy Spirit as the Helper. Using these Bible translations, a wife should help her husband as the Holy Spirit helps the church.

In this chapter, you will read about six diverse marriage relationships, ranging from those that mirrored Bible directives for godly marriage to complete distortions of the marriage relationship. As you read, ponder the couples' behaviors. How do they compare and contrast with God's plans and requirements for a marriage relationship? In these six examples, I wrote first about an ideal marrage and proceeded to the least ideal. You may reorder the sequence as you contemplate and discuss them.

- Manoah and Wife, optimal marriage.
- Amram and Jochebed, famous unknown couple.
- Aquila and Priscilla, early church couple.
- Elkanah and Peninnah, polygamous marriage.
- Zimri and Cozbi, doomed marriage.
- Hosea and Gomer, unloved marriage.

Manoah and Wife, Optimal Marriage (Judges 13–14)

Heart of the Story

The angel of the Lord announced Samson's birth to his parents. The angel appeared first to Samson's mother and then to his father, Manoah.

Story Line

A woman of the Danite tribe was barren. The Bible identified her only as Manoah's wife and Samson's mother. One day, the angel of the

LESSER KNOWN BIBLE CHARACTERS

Lord visited the woman. He told her that she would become pregnant and bear a son. The angel directed the woman to drink no wine or strong drink and eat nothing unclean. Her future son was to be a Nazrite and never cut his hair.

After the angel's visit, Manoah's wife went to her husband. She told him that a Man of God visited her and what the Man said. She didn't realize that the Man was the angel of God. Manoah prayed that the Man would return and teach them how to raise their son.

God responded to Manoah's prayer. The angel appeared to Manoah's wife a second time. Hurriedly, she found her husband and brought him to the angel. Manoah asked the angel how they should manage the child. The angel replied that Manoah's wife should do all that he told her. The angel provided no additional information.

When Manoah invited the angel to eat with him, the angel refused, but suggested that Manoah make a burnt offering to God. As Manoah offered a goat and grain sacrifice on a rock, the angel ascended in the altar flame toward heaven. After the angel ascended, Manoah told his wife that they were going to die because they saw God. Sensibly, his wife responded that if God wanted to kill them, he wouldn't have accepted their burnt offering, showed them these things, and announced the pending birth of a son.

As an adult, Samson went to Timnah where he saw a Philistine woman. When he returned home, Samson told his parents that he wanted the woman for his wife. They asked Samson why he wanted a Philistine wife rather than a woman from his relatives or from his own people. Samson was adamant—he wanted this woman for his wife. The Bible recorded that Manoah, Manoah's wife, and Samson went to Timnah to meet the young woman. Later, they attended the seven-day marriage festival.

Pondering Relationships

God desires affection, even love, in a marriage; however, love alone—in the absence of respect, common values, and similar goals—isn't enough to sustain a marriage. Manoah and his wife had an arranged marriage. Likely, they didn't love each other when they were wed. Maybe, they didn't even know each other. Yet, when we see them in Judges, they are like well-oiled cogs that fit together beautifully. What Manoah lacked, his wife had; what his wife lacked, Manoah had. They brought out the best in each other. Probably, their successful marriage stemmed from their devotion to God. As they trusted and communicated with God, they trusted and communicated with each other.

Manoah's wife didn't keep secrets from her husband. Promptly, she told him about the Man of God's visit. She trusted Manoah and wanted him to share the Man's announcement. Both were ecstatic that after all this time, they were going to have a son.

When Manoah's wife told him that a Man of God announced that she would have a son, Manoah didn't placate his wife with, "Sweetheart, you want a baby so badly that you had a vivid dream." Manoah believed her story. In fact, he believed her so thoroughly that he asked God to send the Man back so they could get more information from him. Not once does the Bible indicate that Manoah wanted a second visit from the angel so he could verify his wife's story.

Both Manoah and his wife were comfortable in their roles. Manoah's words and actions indicated that he was the spiritual head of the household, i.e., he prayed and articulated the significance of seeing God. Manoah's wife thought quickly and rationally; she listed reasons why God wasn't going to kill them. Like many twenty-first-century wives, Manoah's wife wasn't reticent about sharing her thoughts with her husband.

Apparently, the couple was in agreement that Samson shouldn't marry a Philistine. They preferred him to marry a Danite, or at least, an Israelite woman. Neither was aware that their son's motivation for marrying a Philistine was from God. The marriage was part of God's plan for freeing the Israelites from Philistine tyranny.

Reflection

What if Manoah refused to believe that he was the father of his wife's baby? He could have concluded that the male visitor was the future child's father. Would Manoah's disbelief made a difference in the outcome of the story and marriage?

Amram and Jochebed,
Famous Unknown Couple
(Exodus 2:1–10; 6:18–20; Numbers 26:57–58)

Heart of the Story

Moses's father and mother were identified as Amram and Jochebed. The couple was unified in their determination to keep Moses alive.

Story Line

For over 100 years, foreigners, probably the Hykos, ruled Egypt (1652–1542 BC). After expelling them, the Egyptians wanted no foreigners in their country. They feared that Israelite men would join with a foreign nation to reconquer Egypt. The Egyptian pharaoh noted that Israelites were fruitful and multiplied rapidly. He made Israelite men slaves, then, ordered that every Israelite male newborn be thrown into the Nile River to die.

When Moses was born, his parents thought he was beautiful. They couldn't bear to let him drown or be eaten by Nile predators. They agreed to hide Moses in their home. After three months, Moses's cries were loud enough that they could be heard outside their house. Jochebed made a cradle of papyrus reeds and covered it with bitumen and pitch. She lay Moses inside the cradle and placed the cradle into the Nile River. Moses's sister, Miriam, kept watch over the cradle to protect her brother.

Pharaoh's daughter found Moses's cradle floating among the Nile River reeds. Immediately, she recognized him as an Israelite baby. Despite her father's order to kill all Israelite newborn males, she determined to keep the child as her son. Miriam stepped forward and offered to find a wet nurse for the baby. When pharaoh's daughter agreed, Miriam returned with Jochebed. Jochebed acted as Moses's nurse until he was weaned. In ancient times, mothers weaned children when they were between three and four years of age. After Moses was weaned, he went to live with the Egyptian princess.

Pondering Relationships

Both Amram and Jochebed were from the tribe of Levi. Amram means "exalted people," while Jochebed means "the honor of Jehovah." Given their spiritual-sounding names, they were a remnant of Israelites who believed in the God of Abraham, Isaac, and Jacob, despite living in an Egyptian pagan society. Jochebed was Amram's aunt. A marriage between a man and his father's sister was forbidden by Mosaic laws; however, the law didn't exist when Amram married Jochebed.

Amram and Jochebed had a common view of what was right and wrong, i.e., sacrificing their son was wrong, regardless of what the pharaoh ordered. While other Israelite parents allowed male babies to drown, this couple worked together to keep their newborn alive. Their decision endangered their own lives and probably the lives of their other two children, Miriam and Aaron.

As slaves in Egypt, Amram and Jochebed endured horrendous living conditions. Probably, Amram went off to work every morning at slave labor; his days were long. That left Jochebed at home to care for the three children. Initially, Jochebed hid their newborn son. Later, she implemented the couple's plan to save their son's life.

Amram and Jochebed knew that pharaoh's daughter would find Moses if they put the cradle near her bathing site. The question was: What would the princess do? Would she turn their son over to her father's soldiers to be killed, or would she keep the baby? Both parents were prepared for pharaoh's daughter to take their son and rear him. They loved Moses enough to let him be adopted into another culture.

Reflection

A colleague adopted a baby girl from a Central American country. She is a non-Hispanic white and the baby is Hispanic. The baby's mother allowed her baby to be adopted by a person of another race and another nationality. This biological mother knew that her baby daughter would have advantages she could only dream of. Which shows greater parental love, bringing a child up in abject poverty or giving a child for adoption into a different culture and race?

Aquila and Priscilla, Early Church Couple
(Acts 18:2–4, 18–19; 1 Corinthians 16:19)

Heart of the Story

Aquila and Priscilla were Christian converts, friends of Paul, and sensitive in their approach to developing Christians.

Story Line

When Emperor Claudius determined to rid Rome of all Jews, Aquila and Priscilla were exiled from Rome. Probably, they were Christians before they met Paul in Corinth. Like Paul, they were tentmakers. They got along with Paul so well that he lived with them. While in Corinth, Aquila and Priscilla started a Christian church in their home.

When Paul left Corinth for Ephesus, Aquila and Priscilla went with him. At Ephesus, they again started a Christian church. After preaching in Ephesus, Paul left for Antioch. However, Aquila and Priscilla remained in Ephesus. According to Paul, Aquila and Priscilla risked their lives for him. The Bible doesn't document where this event occurred. It may have been in Corinth or Ephesus.

One Sabbath, Aquila and Priscilla heard a visitor, Apollos, speaking in the Ephesus synagogue. Apollos was a learned Jewish scholar from Alexandria, Egypt. He spoke eloquently about the coming Messiah, but knew only the baptism of repentance preached by John. After the synagogue service, Aquila and Priscilla invited Apollos to their home. There, they explained the life and death of Jesus and that he was the expected Messiah. Apollos received their message and became a missionary for Christ.

Pondering Relationships

Aquila and Priscilla shared a common vocation, i.e., tentmakers. Probably, the couple was moderately well-to-do. They appeared to be middle-aged; no children were associated with them. Both loved Christ and helped Paul.

The couple's thoughtfulness is evidenced by their approach to Apollos. Neither confronted him in the Jewish synagogue; neither attempted to embarrass Apollos by their superior knowledge of Christ. Instead, they invited him to their home, probably for a meal. Over the meal, they explained Christ's life, his finished work on the cross, and the baptism of the Holy Spirit. Their considerate approach added a strong voice to spreading the good news of Jesus Christ.

Bible historians identified both Aquila and Priscilla as deacons in the early Christian church. Luke and Paul sometimes referred to the couple as Aquila and Priscilla, and at other times as Priscilla and Aquila.

They had equal status in churches they founded in their home in Corinth and Ephesus.

In Acts, Aquila and Priscilla are stark contrast to Ananias and Sapphira, the first married couple mentioned in the early Christian church. Ananias and Sapphira's love of prominence and money led to the first recorded sin in the church. Aquila and Priscilla modeled how a Christian couple should live.

Reflection

Several years ago, I was in a church home group. One couple was living together but not married. I wish I had modeled Aquila and Priscilla's behavior toward Apollos and invited the couple home for supper. Lovingly, Bruce and I could have identified that sex outside of marriage is a sin. As a Christian, I can't shrug and say, "Well, they're consenting adults," "After all, they're going to get married" or "It's not my job to be judgmental." Is silence consent? When Christians don't speak out about sex outside of marriage, do they condone it?

Elkanah and Peninnah, Polygamous Marriage (1 Samuel 1:1–8)

Heart of the Story

Elkanah married two women, Hannah and Peninnah. Because Elkanah showed Peninnah that he loved Hannah more than her, Peninnah became bitter.

Story Line

Most of us can recite the story of Hannah being barren. We know Hannah prayed for a son. We rejoice with Hannah at the birth of Samuel and admire Hannah for giving Samuel as a precious gift to God. The darker side to this poignant story is that Hannah's husband was a polygamist, who favored one wife over the other.

Elkanah was a Levite who lived in Ephraim. Elkanah's first wife was Hannah. Elkanah loved Hannah, but she was barren. Elkanah married a second woman, Peninnah, in order to father children. Although Peninnah bore Elkanah sons and daughters, he continued to love Hannah best.

When Elkanah went to Shiloh to sacrifice burnt offerings to God, he took his wives and children with him. Each year during the sacrifice, Elkanah gave portions of meat to Peninnah and her sons and daughters. Because he loved Hannah and God closed her womb, Elkanah gave Hannah a double portion of meat.

Peninnah saw Hannah as a rival. She was angry at Hannah and deliberately irritated her. The Bible doesn't specify how Peninnah irritated Hannah; likely, she focused on Hannah's inability to have children.

Pondering Relationships

Can you imagine being a second wife? When your husband wasn't with you at night, you would wonder where he was, whether alone or with his other wife. You would look for signs that he treated her better than you. God never intended for a husband to share his body with more than one woman. Polygamy doesn't mirror God's definition of one flesh.

Peninnah's status as second and least-preferred wife caused her great pain and distress. She wanted Elkanah to love and prefer her. After all, didn't she give Elkanah the children he desired? Her broken heart came out as anger and irritation toward Hannah.

Perhaps, Elkanah overlooked Peninnah's bad behavior toward Hannah because he didn't love Peninnah. He knew he should never have married her. As a Levite, Elkanah was aware of God's plan for a husband-wife relationship to be monogamous. He remembered the conflict that Hagar introduced into Abraham and Sarah's marriage.

Elkanah and Hannah shared a deep faith in God, which created a spiritual bond between them. In contrast, the Bible gave no indication that Peninnah was spiritual. She never took her distress over being the second and least-preferred wife to God. After Samuel's birth, Hannah had three sons and two daughters. At that point, Peninnah didn't even have the solace of being the only wife who gave Elkanah children.

Reflection

Currently, there is a television reality show where a man has four or five (I lost count) wives. Despite the glamor of being on television and dubbed "reality," the show isn't reality. Elkanah's dysfunctional household demonstrated the reality of polygamy. How did Elkanah's marriage to Peninnah pervert God's plan for a husband and wife relationship, i.e., for them to be one flesh?

Zimri and Cozbi, Doomed Marriage
(Numbers 25:6–18; 31:1–8)

Heart of the Story

An Israelite man, Zimri, brought Cozbi, a Midianite princess, to his family in the Israelite camp. When the couple entered the family tent, a priest followed and killed them.

Story Line

Zimri was the son of Salu, a leader in the tribe of Simeon. Cozbi was the daughter of Zur, one of the five Midianite kings. Before the story of Zimri and Cozbi, Israelite judges put to death twenty-four thousand Israelites who worshipped Baal of Peor. Most of the dead Israelites were from the tribe of Simeon. The worship included sacrifices to Baal and having sex with Moabite women. The Israelites believed that the Midianites were in league with the Moabites, who enticed the Israelites to worship Baal.

The Bible didn't record whether Cozbi loved Zimri, or if she was her father's tool to undermine the Israelites. Zimri loved Cozbi. When Zimri brought Cozbi into the Israelite camp, he treated her as a wife. He brought her in front of Moses, the priests, and assembled Israelites. He took her to his family and into the family tent.

Mosaic laws forbid Jewish men from marrying foreign women (Deuteronomy 7:3–4). The Bible doesn't record any conversation between Moses and Zimri when the couple entered the Israelite camp. One commentator suggested that Zimri confronted Moses, asking why Moses could marry a Midianite woman and he couldn't (Lester, 2012). While a shepherd for the Midian priest Jethro, Moses married his daughter.

Pondering Relationships

Despite Zimri and Cozbi's marriage and feelings, Zimri couldn't have chosen a worse time to bring his Midianite princess home. The Israelites were mourning their dead brothers and passionate about pleasing God. They saw Zimri's bringing a Midianite woman into camp as a sign of contempt for God and defiance of Moses's leadership.

Zimri's liaison with Cozbi had political implications. When the Israelites moved, three of the twelve tribes were positioned on each side (north, south, east, and west) of the Tabernacle, located at the center of the marching group. Gad, Reuben, and Simeon guarded the southern flank with Simeon's location on the southeast corner. When Israel made its final march from Moab into the Promised Land, Midianite land was south–southeast of the Israelites. If Zimri and Cozbi's marriage endured, Israel's security could have been compromised by a Midianite enemy among the Simeonites.

The son of an Israelite tribal chief, Zimri had political acumen. He knew the Israelites blamed the deaths of their brethren on foreign women. He understood the importance of security as the Israelites made their final advance into Canaan. Given the mood in the Israelite camp, surely Zimri anticipated some push back when he brought Cozbi home! Zimri was so enthralled by lust for Cozbi that he simply wasn't thinking or acting clearly. Love for God didn't take precedence over Zimri's feelings for Cozbi. Zimri ignored God's words, "You shall have no other gods before me" (Deuteronomy 5:7 NIV).

Reflection

When I was a little girl, I asked Mother who I should love most—she, Daddy, or God. Her response was that I could love whichever one I wanted the most. Mother was wrong. I am to love God most and put my love for him ahead of my love for anyone else. God is the foundational relationship on which all others rest. If I don't get love right with God, I likely won't get it right with my parents or spouse. Draw a diagram of relationships in your life, i.e., God, your spouse, children, boss, and any other important recipient of your loyalty. Does it show that you honor God above anyone else? Do you need to alter any relationship in the diagram?

Hosea and Gomer, Unloved Marriage
(Hosea 1–3)

Heart of the Story

At God's direction, the prophet Hosea married a harlot. The marriage was notably unsuccessful. Yet, it accurately depicted God's relationship with the idolatrous Israelites.

Story Line

Hosea and Gomer lived in Israel about the middle of the eighth century BC during the reign of Jeroboam II. Hosea was a prophet of God. When God ordered Hosea to marry an adulterous woman, he married Gomer.

Gomer was an unfaithful wife and mother of three children. Possibly, Hosea was the father of the first son, or none of the children. Believing that other men could give her more physical comforts and ornaments than Hosea, Gomer left Hosea. She abandoned her children. After all, children would only curtail her wanton lifestyle! Gomer took lovers and prostituted herself.

Eventually, living as a prostitute palled. Gomer realized that her life as Hosea's wife was better than how she currently lived. Possibly, Gomer lost her looks or her freshness. Unthinking or uncaring that she hurt and embarrassed Hosea, Gomer asked him if she could return to his home. Hosea refused to take Gomer back into his household. Hosea's decision was okay with God. The Bible provided no indication that God gave Hosea other directions at that point. Gomer became destitute. She had no option but to sell herself into slavery so she would have somewhere to live and food to eat.

Pondering Relationship

Gomer was self-centered. She had little, if any, affection for Hosea. She was unfaithful to Hosea when she lived as his wife, and after she left him and the children. Gomer only wanted to return to Hosea for her own comfort.

When God told Hosea to marry an adulterous woman, he didn't direct Hosea to love the woman. In ancient Israel, kinship regulated marriage. Possibly, Gomer was a cousin or second cousin to Hosea. Relative or not, marriage to a harlot brought great shame on Hosea's entire family. Shame multiplied when the family learned that Gomer was unfaithful and left Hosea.

In Hosea 3:1, God told Hosea, not only to purchase Gomer from her slave owner, but to love her. Only at this point did God require Hosea to engage his emotions. He must love a woman who left him for lovers! For Hosea, loving Gomer was harder than marrying her.

After Hosea purchased Gomer from slavery, he provided clear boundaries for their life together: Gomer would be betrothed to Hosea for many days, during which time, she wouldn't prostitute herself or have sex with another man. Hosea would act the same toward Gomer until she proved her loyalty to him. Only then would marital relations be resumed. Hosea wasn't about to engage his emotions until he had evidence that Gomer changed her lifestyle and was prepared to be a loyal wife.

Reflection

We don't know if Hosea and Gomer's husband-wife relationship was ever rebuilt; but, Hosea outlined a plan to repair the marriage. What does it take for a marriage relationship dulled by unfaithfulness to be restored?

Contemplation[1]

"It takes two to tango" is an American proverb. Its application goes well beyond couples dancing. In marriage most of us tango, or interact, in the same way that our parent's interacted. What happens if they had a dysfunctional, non-Christian marriage? Likely, we follow their example in our own marriage. We know no other way to behave. Remember the verse, "But seek his kingdom, and these things will be given to you as well" (Luke 12:31 NIV). When individuals seek, find, and follow God, usually they are mature enough for a Christian marriage.

Pondering Marriage Relationships

1. From chapter 1, did you get any instructions that could enhance your marriage relationship? What did you learn?
2. Did you feel rebuked for one or more of your behaviors? Which ones? What can you change in your behavior so it more closely mirrors God's requirements for a godly spouse and a godly marriage relationship?

---

1   No marriages between two men or two women were included in this chapter because none were found in the Bible. What do you make of this finding?

Chapter 2

Fathers and Daughters

Ancient Israelite parents valued children and believed they were a gift from God. Fathers wanted sons to help care for flocks, farm their land, and construct buildings. At the same time, fathers loved daughters. Often girls were gentle and affectionate and looked to a father's comfort. Unlike some ancient and twenty-first-century societies, Israelite parents didn't kill newborn girls. Extremely poor fathers could sell prepubescent daughters as slaves; however, strict Israelite laws govern their care and redemption.

Fathers were responsible for protecting and providing for daughters. In ancient Israel, a girl married at about twelve to thirteen years of age, after she reached puberty and started menstruating. By then, she was ready to live with a husband, have children, and manage a household. Fathers selected husbands for daughters. Generally, husbands were a few years older than wives, but at times they were a decade, or more, older. Ideally, girls married first cousins; thus, daughters remained close to parents and siblings. A groom's father paid the bride's father a fee—*mohar* or "bride price"—to compensate for the daughter's loss to her birth family. For the most part, dowries were a New Testament concept not practiced among ancient Israelites.

Ancient Israel was a patriarchal society. The father's many responsibilities to children were outlined in Mosaic law. Fathers were responsible to instruct girls, as well as boys, in righteous behavior. Specifically, fathers taught God's words to children when they sat in their homes, before bedtime, when they got up in the morning, and when they walked along the road, e.g., visited family or neighbors. Israelites believed that if they trained young children in the ways of God, children would continue to live righteous lives when they were older.

God expected fathers to set an example for children; their own actions must be right and just. Israelite fathers were required to show children the same compassion that God showed them. In the New Testament, Christian fathers were directed not to exasperate (irritate, provoke), embitter, or otherwise discourage children.

Although fathers were responsible for daughters before they married, daughters were accountable for following applicable Mosaic laws. For example, daughters should worship God and have no other gods, i.e., household gods. Daughters should honor both father and mother and refrain from eating forbidden foods. They were to keep themselves pure and free from sexual sins. Daughters could make vows to God as long as their fathers didn't object. When a man had no sons, daughters inherited his property.

In ancient cultures, mothers and daughters spent more time together; however, the most important relationship in a girl's life was with her father. From this relationship, she learned to respect men, to include her future husband. She learned her worth as an individual and that her opinions and desires mattered. In the upcoming chapter, you will read six relationships between fathers and daughters. The six relationships move from the most loving to the most abhorrent. See what you think of these lesser known Bible father-daughter dyads:

- Jairus's young daughter.
- Acsah, a beloved daughter.
- Daughters of Zelophehad, a deceased father.
- Jephthah's sacrificed daughter.
- Dinah and Tamar, daughters of unfaithful fathers.
- Lot, father of immoral daughters.

Jairus's Young Daughter
(Mark 5:22–24, 35–43)

Heart of the Story

Jairus loved his daughter enough to risk criticism from the Jewish elite by asking a young rabbi, Jesus, to heal her. Possibly, Jairus even believed that Jesus could raise his daughter from the dead.

Story Line

Jairus was a ruler of a synagogue, which is similar to a church administrator today. He was a layman, responsible for looking after the buildings and supervising worship. Jairus had one daughter, a twelve-year-old, who became ill. The Bible didn't record how long she was ill; but, by this story, she was in critical condition.

Desperate to save his daughter's life, Jairus found Jesus, fell at his feet, and pleaded with him to heal his daughter. Jairus was relieved and happy when Jesus said he would go to Jairus's house and heal her. Likewise, he must have been anxious when Jesus stopped to heal a woman. Possibly, he wanted to tug at Jesus's hand and say, "Please, please, let's go! My daughter is really, really sick."

Then, the unthinkable happened. Men arrived from Jairus's house and told Jairus that his beloved daughter was dead. No doubt, Jairus wanted to wail with grief. Immediately, Jesus told Jairus to not be afraid and to believe. He continued walking toward Jairus's home. In the time it took to reach his house, Jairus was hoping—more than believing—that the men were wrong about his daughter's death. Could this young rabbi do something—anything—to ensure that his daughter lived?

When Jesus arrived at Jairus's home, the household was loudly mourning the daughter's death. Jesus entered the home. Before he even looked at the girl, Jesus declared that she wasn't dead but merely asleep. Jesus put everyone but Jairus, his wife, and disciples out of the house. Then, he went to where the child lay, took her by the hand, and said, "Little girl, I say to you, get up!" (Mark 5:41 NIV). Immediately, Jairus's daughter stood up and walked around. Jesus directed the parents to feed her. He gave them strict orders to tell no one that he healed the girl.

Pondering Relationships

Jairus loved his daughter and didn't care who knew it. No doubt he contacted the best physicians in the Capernaum area to heal her; but, they couldn't heal the girl. Probably, Jairus had synagogue priests make special sacrifices for his daughter's health. Priests may have come to his home and prayed for the girl.

For Jairus to seek out an itinerant rabbi was noteworthy. Most synagogue elite actively opposed or discounted Jesus. Jairus didn't care what they thought. He focused on his beloved daughter and how to get her healed. After Jesus touched the young girl and told her to get up, immediately she started to walk around. There was no period of convalescence where she gradually got her strength back. Likely, both Jairus and her mother hugged her so tightly that she had little chance to move.

Although Jairus's daughter was twelve years old, Jesus called her a "little girl." Perhaps, her stature was small and she wasn't yet into puberty. No doubt, Jairus spoke Hebrew and Greek; but, Jesus spoke to the girl in Aramaic. Aramaic was the common language spoken in the Holy Land in the first century AD. Because the child was female, most likely, she had no formal schooling and never learned Greek or Hebrew. Jesus cared that the child understand his words.

Few things are tenderer than a father's love for a young daughter. Often the father is large and muscular, while his daughter is small and fragile. He has learned to handle his daughter with care and to modulate his voice, even when reprimanding her. Jairus was a kind father, and Jesus knew it. Jesus honored and reinforced Jairus's love for his only daughter.

As Jairus's daughter grew into a woman, she would hear the story of her father defying synagogue authority and custom to save her life. Of course, she would be grateful to the young rabbi for healing her; but, most of all, she would remember how much her father loved her. Her important father fell at the feet and begged a young rabbi to save her life. Her father's valuation of her influenced her self-worth.

Reflection

The way that Jairus loved his daughter is the same way that our heavenly Father loves us. How would you describe God's love for you? Does God consider you fragile?

Acsah, Beloved Daughter
(Joshua 15:13–19)

Heart of the Story

Caleb loved his daughter, Acsah, enough to give her a strong husband, land, and springs of water in the desert. Acsah was confident enough of her father's love to ask for a special favor.

Story Line

When Joshua administered the division of the Promised Land in Canaan, Caleb asked for the land around Hebron. He reminded Joshua that Moses said he could have that land. After Joshua granted the land to Caleb, he immediately began to wrest it from the Anakites. Caleb promised his daughter, Acsah, to the man who captured Debir, a key Anakite town. When his nephew, Othniel, took the city, Caleb gave Acsah to Othniel in marriage. Othniel was the first Israelite judge. He won military victories that brought peace to Israel for forty years. Caleb secured his beloved daughter a strong husband.

After Acsah and Othniel married, Acsah urged Othniel to ask Caleb for a certain field. Caleb granted Othniel's request. Then, Acsah went to Caleb and asked her father for a special favor. Because Caleb gave Othniel land in the Negev Desert, would Caleb give her springs of water to go with the land? Caleb's response was to give Acsah both an upper and lower spring.

Pondering Relationships

Caleb was eighty-five years old when Joshua assigned him land at Hebron. Probably, Caleb had several daughters; but, for some reason, Acsah was special to him. Perhaps, she was his youngest child. Both respected and loved each other. Acsah didn't protest when Caleb used her as the prize for capturing an Anakite town.

Notice, it was Acsah, not Othinel, who initiated Othinel asking Caleb for land. Acsah was sure that her father would give the land to Othniel. When Acsah urged Othinel to ask for the land, probably her arguments were rational and persuasive. Even though Othinel was a noted warrior, asking his father-in-law for land would have been difficult. On his own initiative, Othinel wouldn't have made this request of Caleb.

When Acsah asked her father for water to go with the land he gave Othniel, she traveled from her home to Caleb without Othniel. As Acsah arrived at Caleb's location, Caleb met her before she was off her donkey. Caleb even asked Acsah what he could do for her!

Land with year-around water, such as springs, were exceptionally valuable in the Negev Desert area. An upper and lower spring meant that one spring was located at a higher elevation and one at a lower elevation. Livestock in both locations would have ready access to water. Even if one spring dried up, the other might continue to flow. The two springs added to the wealth of Othniel's family and increased Acsah's value to her husband.

Generally, the first man an Israelite daughter knew was her father. A healthy, close father-daughter relationship showed a girl that men were caring, strong, and protective. A father was a daughter's role model for what to expect from men, particularly her husband. Caleb reared a confident daughter, who was a confident wife.

Reflection

How do fathers demonstrate their love to adult daughters, even newly married daughters, in the twenty-first century? In your relationship with your daughter, are you encouraging her to view herself as worthy?

Daughters of a Deceased Father
(Numbers 27:1–11; Numbers 36:1–12; Joshua 17:1–6)

Heart of the Story

After Zelophehad died, his five daughters petitioned Moses to receive his portion of the Promised Land. God ordered that the daughters be given the land, instituting a new inheritance law in Israel.

Story Line

Zelophehad's five daughters were Mahlah, Noah, Hoglah, Milcah, and Tirzah. They belonged to the tribe of Manasseh. The Bible doesn't name their mother; perhaps she was deceased. The story took place while the Israelites camped on the Moab plain, before crossing the Jordan River into the Promised Land.

The five daughters approached the tent of meeting and stood before Moses and the entire assembly. They began their petition by reminding Moses that their father died in the desert. Quickly, they pointed out that Zelophehad wasn't part of Korah's rebellion. The daughters said that because Zelophehad died without leaving a son, his name would disappear from his clan. They requested that Moses give them Zelophehad's assigned portion of the Promised Land.

Moses took the daughters' case before God, who ruled that Zelophehad's assigned property and inheritance should be given to his daughters. Thus, God instituted a new inheritance law for the Israelites. The new Israelite inheritance law was that if a man died and left no son, his inheritance should be given to his daughters. A later ruling stipulated that the daughters must marry within their own tribe.

Pondering Relationships

The Bible provides little information on Zelophehad. His daughters told Moses that their father died for his own sin. Possibly, Zelophehad's sin was his belief forty years earlier that the Israelites couldn't conquer the Promised Land. Alternatively, Jewish rabbi Akiva and Midrashic literature proposed that Zelophehad was the man who gathered kindling on the Sabbath day (Hareuveni, 1989). By order of God, the Sabbath breaker was stoned to death (Numbers 15:32–36).

Whatever the cause of Zelophehad's death, he instilled solidarity, courage, and determination into his daughters. Taking no action on behalf of their father's name and themselves would have been easier and according to Israelite custom. Approaching the entire Israelite assembly and requesting Moses to change the Israelite inheritance laws was beyond difficult. Zelophehad's daughters were five fatherless girls in a man's world. Part of their motivation was their realization that without property, unmarried daughters were reduced to poverty, even to slavery or prostitution.

Zelophehad's daughters worked within the system to secure their father's property rights. Working within the customs of the culture gave traction to their request. The girls pointed out how the proposed request was consistent with current tribal and national beliefs. Neither viewers nor judges felt disconnected from cultural values, even though changes were requested.

Zelophehad was the role model for his daughter's courage and tact. Given the girls' behavior, I doubt Zelophehad gathered wood on the Sabbath day, despite Rabbi Akiva's suggestion. Through the daughters' initiative, Israelite women achieved property rights; however, they still weren't equal recipients of Yahweh's promise. When a woman married, property she owned became her husband's. The daughters of Zelophehad obeyed Moses and married their cousins. Their property transferred to their cousins. The property didn't leave the tribe of Manasseh.

Reflection

Do fathers have responsibility to plan for a daughter's secure growth and development? What happens to that responsibility if a father dies and there are still daughters at home?

Jephthah's Sacrificed Daughter
(Judges 11)

Heart of the Story

Jephthah vowed that if God gave him victory over the Ammonites, he would sacrifice whatever came out of his door first. The first person who exited his door was Jephthah's only daughter.

Story Line

The three Israelite tribes that settled east of the Jordan River were Reuben, Gad, and half the tribe of Manasseh. Collectively, this area was known as Gilead. At the time of this story, Gilead was overrun by the Ammonites, who oppressed the eastern tribes for eighteen years. Previous Israelite history showed that God selected judges to free the Israelites from foreign suppression and tyranny, e.g., Barak with King Jabin; however, the Gileadites didn't ask God for a judge. Instead, they recruited a judge to lead their army.

Jephthah's father was Gilead, a member of Manasseh. Although his mother was a prostitute, Gilead reared Jephthah in his home. At some point, perhaps after Gilead died, Jephthah's half brothers expelled him from the family home. Jephthah went to Tob, Syria, where he became the leader of a group of adventurers.

Unable to find anyone to lead their army against the Ammonites, the Gileadites asked Jephthah to be their commander. Jephthah agreed without asking God what he should do. His chief concern was getting a promise from the Gileadites that he would be their peacetime leader as well as their wartime commander. Jephthah wasn't about to have his brother's drive him out again, particularly after he fought the Ammonites for them.

Before Jephthah engaged the Ammonites in battle, he approached God. He promised God, "If you give the Ammonites into my hands, whatever comes out of the door of my house to meet me when I return in triumph over the Ammonites will be the Lord's, and I will sacrifice it as a burnt offering" (Judges 11:31 NIV). This vow is the first time Jephthah talked to God about being Gilead's judge.

Likely, Jephthah won a decisive victory over the Ammonites, not because he made a vow of sacrifice to God, but because God's plan was to free Gileadites from Ammonite oppression.

After his military victory, Jephthah returned home. The first person out his door was his beloved daughter.

Pondering Relationships

The Bible didn't name Jephthah's daughter; however, she was Jephthah's only child. Probably, she was in her early teens. She was a virgin and wasn't betrothed. When Jepthah's daughter saw him returning home, she ran out the door. In joy over his victory, she danced toward him, playing a tambourine. As Jephthah saw his daughter, he realized she was the first person out his door. He remembered his vow to God. Immediately, Jephthah was filled with anguish; he tore his clothes in grief.

Jephthah loved his daughter. He cried that she made him miserable and wretched. Jephthah's words sounded like he blamed his daughter for the heartbreaking outcome of his rash vow. At no point did Jephthah show remorse for making a vow that included human sacrifice—an action detestable to God.

When she learned of Jephthah's vow, his daughter's response was remarkable; she didn't resist. Instead, she encouraged Jephthah to keep his vow to God. Clearly, Jephthah's daughter believed in the true God of Israel. Her only request was that Jephthah allow her two months to roam the hills and weep with her friends because she would never marry. After two months, Jephthah's daughter returned from the hills. Presumably, Jephthah sacrificed her, as he promised God.

Recent Bible commentators suggested that Jephthah didn't kill his daughter, but gave her as a living sacrifice to God. As such, she would have remained unmarried throughout her life. Whether she was physically sacrificed or lived as an unmarried woman, Jephthah lost his opportunity to secure a dynasty of leadership over the men of Giliead, his old adversaries.

Jephthah's daughter's compliance is reminiscent of Acsah, when Caleb announced she would become the wife of the man who captured Debir. The major difference between the two father-daughter dyads was their fathers' behavior. Caleb was a wise leader, who put his confidence and trust in God. Jephthah was impulsive and trusted himself. Acsah could depend on her father's actions. In contrast, Jephthah's daughter couldn't rely on her father to look out for her present or future.

Reflection

What would Jephthah have done if his beloved daughter begged him not to sacrifice her? What, if anything, do you think Jephthah learned from this experience?

Dinah and Tamar,
Daughters of Unfaithful Fathers
(Genesis 34; 2 Samuel 13:1–22)

Heart of the Story

At least twice in the Bible, fathers did nothing in response to daughters being raped.

Story Line

After Jacob entered Canaan, he bought land from Hamor, king of Shechem, and camped on it. Jacob and Leah's daughter, Dinah, went out to visit the women who lived there. Hamor's son, Prince Shechem, saw Dinah. Shechem took Dinah and violated her. After the rape, Shechem loved Dinah and kept her with him. He wanted to marry Dinah. Shechem asked King Hamor to secure Dinah for his wife.

Genesis doesn't tell us how Jacob felt when he heard Dinah was raped; however, her brothers (Reuben, Simeon, Levi, and Judah) were furious. Using trickery, they killed King Hamor and Prince Shechem. The brothers took Dinah from Shechem's house back to Jacob's tents. Jacob's response to his son's actions was to tell them that they made him a stench to the Canaanites.

King David's son, crown prince Amnon, lusted after Tamar. He couldn't possess her because she was a virgin and his half sister. Tamar was the daughter of King David and his wife Maacah. Eventually, Amnon pretended to be ill. When David visited him, Amnon asked that Tamar prepare and serve him bread. On David's orders, Tamar went to Amnon's quarters. After Tamar prepared and served bread to Amnon, he assaulted her. Despite Tamar's poignant pleas to stop, Amnon overpowered and raped her. After the rape, Amnon hated Tamar. He expelled her from his rooms. Weeping, Tamar went to her brother Absalom's house rather than return to the royal palace. Absalom calmed Tamar and offered her a home with him.

When King David learned that Prince Amnon raped Tamar, he was furious; yet, similar to Jacob, David took no action on his daughter's behalf. Two years later, Absalom used a ruse to get Amnon to his country home. There, Absalom killed Amnon in retaliation for his rape of Tamar.

Pondering Relationships

When Jacob lived, there were no written Israelite laws against rape; however, God would have instilled in Jacob his moral law that rape was wrong. King David knew the Mosaic laws about sex with a relative and the penalty if a man raped a woman. These Mosaic laws included that a man shouldn't have sexual relations with the daughter of his father's wife. If he did, the man should be cut off from his people. Further, if a man raped a virgin who wasn't pledged to be married, he must marry the girl. King David should have exiled Amnon from the Israelite community, or at a minimum, required him to marry Tamar.

After the rapes, Dinah's and Tamar's life changed drastically. That they were raped was common knowledge. A young Israelite woman who wasn't a virgin was unmarriageable. After Dinah was returned to Jacob's home, she is mentioned one other time in the Bible. She was one of the individuals who entered Egypt with Jacob. Beautiful, naive Tamar lived as a desolate woman in Absalom's home. No husband was associated with either Dinah's or Tamar's name.

The Bible provides no evidence that either father consoled their daughters for the rape inflicted on them. The reason the two fathers didn't respond to their daughter's rape is perplexing. Several scholars suggested that Dinah's behavior led to her being raped, i.e., Dinah was complicit in Shechem violating her. However, Genesis is clear: Shechem "took and violated" Dinah (Genesis 34:2 NIV).

Possibly, Jacob's and David's decision to withhold justice for their daughters was based on guilt and fear. Jacob blamed himself for settling among a people who had no qualms about raping a neighbor's daughter. Jacob was afraid of the combined might of the Canaanites and Perizzites. He thought that if he refused to let Shechem have Dinah, war could erupt and destroy his household. Further, Jacob reprimanded Dinah's brothers for avenging her honor.

Similarly, King David must have felt tremendous guilt for ordering Tamar to Amnon's home. He put Tamar in the position to be violated; but, David was afraid that exiling Prince Amnon would destabilize his dynasty and Israel's throne. Not long before, David had Bathsheba's husband killed so he could marry her. David's behavior strained the loyalty of his soldiers, commanders, and subjects. David didn't want to remind anyone of his own sin.

Dinah and Tamar were victims of their fathers' fears and ambitions. They were powerless pawns of their male relatives. Although both Jacob and King David are heroes of the Bible, their behavior toward their daughters isn't admirable. Neither Dinah nor Tamar grew into the woman she could have been if her father obtained justice for her. Justice doesn't always right a wrong; however, justice has the power to heal grief (Adeyamo, 2006).

Reflection

How did Jacob and David's failure to obtain justice for their daughters lead to more violence in their families? Did either Jacob or David have a responsibility to find husbands for their daughters?

Lot, Father of Immoral Daughters
(Genesis 19:30–38)

Heart of the Story

After the destruction of Sodom, Lot took his two daughters to live in a cave in the hills. There, Lot was raped by both daughters while he lay drunk.

Story Line

Lot was Abraham's nephew. After separating from Abraham, Lot lived on a fertile plain, which included Sodom, Gomorrah, and Zoar. Lot married, sired two daughters, and moved into Sodom. The Bible doesn't give the names of Lot's wife or daughters. Sodom was known for its depraved wickedness; nonetheless, Lot arranged for his daughters to marry townsmen.

Before the daughters were married, two angels visited Sodom. Thinking the angels were travelers, Lot insisted that they stay in his home. That evening, men of Sodom surrounded Lot's house. They demanded that Lot bring the two men outside so they could have sex with them. Lot begged the townsmen not to defile his guests. He offered his two virgin daughters to the Sodomites in place of the travelers. When the Sodomites attempted to take the two visitors by force, the angels struck them blind.

The angels directed Lot to flee the city. Sodom was so wicked that God was going to destroy it. Lot believed the angels. He went to his future sons-in-law and asked them to flee with him. Both refused, thinking that Lot was joking. When dawn came, the angels led Lot's family from Sodom. They warned Lot and his family not to look back or to stop anywhere on the plain. Afraid that disaster would overtake the family while they were out in the open, Lot asked the angels if they could go to Zoar. The angels agreed and promised not to destroy the small town. In the process of fleeing Sodom, Lot's wife looked back. She became a pillar of salt.

Later, Lot moved himself and his daughters to a cave in the hills. The Bible doesn't tell readers how long Lot and his daughters lived in the cave; however, eventually, the daughters became concerned about preserving their family line. On separate nights, a daughter got Lot drunk and raped him. Both became pregnant by their father. The older daughter had a son whom she named Moab. He became father of the Moabites. The younger daughter's son was named Ben Ammi, the father of the Ammonites. These two tribes became the worst enemies of the Israelites.

Pondering Relationships

In the ancient Near East, fathers were responsible for finding husbands for daughters. After his daughters' prospective husbands perished in Sodom, Lot should have looked for other mates for his daughters. We aren't sure why Lot didn't go to Abraham or into Zoar to find husbands for the two girls. Possibly, Lot was ashamed to go to Abraham after living among the wicked Sodomites. The Zoarans may have associated Lot with the destruction of Sodom and Gomorrah. They didn't want Lot's daughters in their families.

Likely, Lot was deeply depressed over the loss of his wife, home, and wealth. He had little energy to find husbands for his daughters. Often, depression is associated with overconsumption of alcohol. Lot's routine was to drink wine at night. He was so drunk on at least two nights that he didn't know his daughters had sex with him.

Lot's daughters acted outside most cultural norms. Each decided she wanted a son to protect and provide for her future. Their plan to get Lot drunk and rape him was sound, even if perverted. If one or both daughters had a female child, they would use Lot a second or third time.

We don't know if Lot taught his daughters to love and fear God; however, the Bible says Lot was a righteous man tormented by the filthy lives of men he lived among (2 Peter 2:7–8). At the same time, Lot chose to live in Sodom and rear his daughters there. A personal righteous life and a godly upbringing isn't always enough to guide children. They need contact with godly people (Adeyemo, 2006).

Reflection

How did Lot fail to meet God's standards and cultural expectations for a father-daughter relationship? Do you have additional insights to explain the daughter's perverted behavior?

Contemplation

Most Christian fathers want a daughter to know he loves her as much as Jairus loved his daughter or Caleb loved Acsah. The only way a daughter will know she is loved by her father is if he demonstrates that love. Simply saying "I love you" has little value. Remember the old saying, "Your actions speak so loud, I can't hear what you say"? Fathers who participate in a daughter's life, e.g., soccer practice, band concerts, show they love her. A father who isn't involved in a daughter's life still impacts it. That daughter looks for a husband who is the opposite of her father.

When I left for college, my father shook my hand and wished me well. In many families, the norm for a father-daughter relationship is not a hug and kiss good-bye, but a wave or handshake. Not having a warm, loving relationship with a father hampers a daughter's and a woman's relationship with God. These girls/women have difficulty understand the depth and breadth of the heavenly Father's love because their earthly father never demonstrated love.

Can you imagine Christ, who loves you unbelieveably, shaking hands with you if you left for a long absence? True, Christ never leaves us. But if he did, he would hug and kiss us good-bye. God is never reluctant to demonstrate love for his daughters.

Pondering Father-Daughter Relationships:

1. When a husband and wife divorces, how can a father remain a part of his daughter's life? How can both the daughter's mother and father contribute to a father's needed role in a daughter's life?

2. Psychologists tell us that a daughter who doesn't receive love and positive reinforcement from her father may seek male attention elsewhere. Sometimes this attention-seeking behavior isn't healthy and is even promiscuous. Have you seen or heard of a situation like this? What can be done to head off this least-preferred outcome for daughters?

CHAPTER 3

Mothers and Sons

Mothers leave an indelible imprint on son's lives. Often a man takes his mother's unwritten rules into his own family and job. These rules influence the way he relates to his wife, daughters, and women coworkers. For sons to grow into successful men, they require three things from mothers: to be respected, needed, and fulfilled (Leman, 2012).

- Respected. A son must know that he pleases his mother, and she sees him as capable and worthy. A son needs his mother to demonstrate that he has a solid place in her heart, home, and world.

- Needed. Often when a son is young, he sees his mother as super-capable. A mother should show she needs her son's assistance. She can allow even a young boy to problem-solve, compete, and conquer around the house.

- Fulfilled. Mothers should affirm a son's maleness and train him in biblical behavior and gender norms. Even when playing games, a mother should never allow a son to debase her as a woman or person.

Bible mothers were proactive, decisive women. They willingly fought for their son's life and well-being. Mothers called out prophets and kings to get right treatment for sons. They comforted sons. They couldn't forget the son they birthed and breast-fed. Even after Rizpah's sons, Armoni and Mephibosheth, were murdered, she confronted feral animals to keep their bodies from being dismembered. Often when the Bible depicted the depth of a mother's love for her child, it was an illustration for the love that God had for Israel and Christian believers.

The Bible contains little information about how a son should treat his mother; however, what it says is emphatic. In both Testaments, children are exhorted to obey, respect, and honor mothers and to be subject to both fathers and mothers. The "Sayings of the Wise" (Proverbs) include that a son shouldn't neglect his mother's instruction or despise her when she is old. Foolish sons bring grief and uncorrected children bring disgrace to mothers. When sons have a noble mother, they stand and call her blessed.

With the exception of King Lemuel and Solomon, Bible sons gave little indication that they valued their mothers. Sons were often passive recipients of mother's actions rather than proactive and decisive. Few, if any, resisted their mother's actions.

Unlike the marriages in chapter 1 and the father-daughter relationships in chapter 2, the six vignettes in chapter 3 are difficult to fit on a continuum from most to least optimal. You may want to resequence them based on your thinking. As you read these six stores, evaluate whether or not each mother loved her son and met his needs. Did sons meet the Bible's criteria for honorable treatment of their mother? The six mother-son stories are:

- Mother's advice to King Lemuel
- Lois, Eunice, and Timothy
- Zipporah and sons
- Shunammite woman's son
- Queen Ano's dying son
- Murder of Rizpah's sons

Mother's Advice to King Lemuel
(Proverbs 31:1–9)

Heart of the Story

A mother gave advice to her son Lemuel, a future king. King Lemuel valued her advice so highly that he put it in writing.

Story Line

These nine verses are the only reference to Lemuel in the Bible. In Hebrew, Lemuel means "devoted to God." The proverbs (or oracle) were uttered by Lemuel's mother, who in ancient times was called the queen mother. Often, the queen mother was the most influential woman in a monarch's court.

Some scholars believe that these proverbs were recorded by Solomon; therefore, the advice came from his mother, Bathsheba. Most associate the verses with King Lemuel of Massa. Massa was a country in northern Arabia. Given this country, King Lemuel would have been a non-Israelite. Perhaps, the king's origin isn't as important as the proverbs' advice and the way they described the mother-son relationship.

The queen mother begins by identifying Lemuel as the son of her womb whom she dedicated to God. Her words indicate genuine love and concern for him. Lemuel's mother ponders what advice she should give her son so he will reign well. This verse reminds us that it is not only fathers and teachers who have a responsibility to instruct children about God's precepts. Mothers play a key role in explaining and clarifying God's laws to children.

The queen mother's subsequent words of advice are written in the imperative mood. We hear insistence in the warnings to Lemuel that he avoid promiscuity and drunkenness. Possibly, avoiding promiscuity was related to not keeping a large harem, a common practice in the Middle East. Explicitly, the queen mother advises Lemuel to avoid drunkenness, lest he pervert the rights of the afflicted.

The final two proverbs are a call to action. The queen mother wants Lemuel to be an advocate for the rights of individuals who have no voice of their own, i.e., the destitute. She advises Lemuel to open his mouth—as opposed to remaining silent—and to judge rightly! Lemuel must be a responsible spokesman for the poor and needy.

Pondering Relationships

The queen mother is definite in her advice to Lemuel. Unhesitatingly, she asserted her beliefs, confident that Lemuel wouldn't retaliate against her outspokenness. This kind of familiarity suggested that she was part of Lemuel's life since childhood. She didn't start giving advice when he ascended to the throne.

Likely, Lemuel's mother didn't speak all the proverbs at the same time. She gave discrete advice as Lemuel developed and was ready to apply the knowledge, e.g., don't give your strength to women whose ways will destroy kings. Whatever the time frame of his mother's advice, Lemuel treasured it. Only an individual who wanted to remember and follow his mother's advice would record it. The queen mother's advice was deemed so important to kingly rule that it became a part of holy scriptures in a country far from Massa.

The renowned Christian family psychologist and author, Kevin Leman (2012), asserted that a mother is the most important figure in a boy's life. The proverbs of King Lemuel support Leman's assertion. King Lemuel didn't record any of his father's teachings; but, he lived by his mother's words.

Reflection

What advice from you do you want your son to remember and follow? Write it down; consider when to give each piece to your son.

Lois, Eunice, and Timothy
(Acts 14:5, 19–23; Acts 16:1–3;
2 Timothy 1:3–7)

Heart of the Story

Timothy's life was influenced by his grandmother and mother. Lois and Eunice demonstrated the positive influence of a godly grandmother and mother on a son's life.

Story Line

During his first missionary journey (AD 46–49), Paul went to Lystra, a town now located in Turkey. In 6 BC, Caesar Augustus designated Lystra a Roman colony. Many Roman soldiers retired there. Despite Rome's influence, native Lystrans spoke their local language, Lycoania. Many worshipped the Greek pantheon of gods, e.g., Zeus and Hermes.

A Jewish woman, Lois lived in Lystra. Her daughter, Eunice, was Timothy's mother. Eunice married a Greek man who was a pagan. According to Jewish law, a child of a Jewish mother is a Jew even if the father is non-Jewish. Although a Jew, Timothy wasn't circumcised.

Both Lois and Eunice were devout Jews and taught Timothy Jewish beliefs. Because of their close association and the role both had in Timothy's upbringing, possibly, Lois lived with Eunice. Lois, Eunice, and Timothy heard Paul's message of Christ and converted to Christianity. Eunice's Greek husband didn't convert.

While Paul was preaching in Lystra, Jews came from Antioch and Iconium. They incited the townspeople against Paul and Barnabas. The crowd stoned Paul and dragged him outside Lystra, where he was left for dead. After the disciples gathered around him, Paul got up. Probably, Timothy was one of the disciples, as were Lois and Eunice.

The next day, Paul and Barnabas left Lystra to continue their missionary journey. Despite personal danger, they returned from their journey through Lystra. In Lystra, they appointed elders for the new church. The Lystran church didn't meet in Lois and Eunice's home, probably because

Eunice's husband was a Greek. Timothy wasn't a church elder. At this time in the early Christian church, not being circumcised was an impediment to being designated an elder. Further, Timothy was young in years and in the Christian faith.

Pondering Relationships

Timothy was a product of a mixed marriage, i.e., a Greek father and a Jewish mother. Timothy's Greek father played an insignificant role in his religious upbringing. Until Paul took an interest in him, Lois and Eunice were the primary spiritual guides in Timothy's life. Timothy had frequent physical ailments. His character was a blend of amiability and natural reserve, coupled with faithfulness in spite of timidity. Possibly, Timothy learned some of these behaviors from watching how the two Jewish women behaved in a Greek household.

Timothy was an important figure in the first-century Christian church. He accompanied Paul on his second missionary journey. Often, Timothy was Paul's official representative to early Christian churches. Timothy was the recipient of two letters from Paul, which are part of the canon of the New Testament. In Paul's letters to the young churches, he mentioned Timothy more times than any other companion. He called Timothy his "spiritual son."

Probably, it was good for Timothy to leave Lois and Eunice and travel with Paul. Although his grandmother and mother were fine Christian women, his father was "MIA" (missing in action) as a source of influence. A strong male figure, such as Paul, balanced the female influences in Timothy's life.

Reflection

How would you define Timothy's relationship with Lois and Eunice? How were Lois, Eunice, and Timothy examples of the importance of intergenerational faith?

Zipporah and Sons
(Exodus 2:16–22, 4:18–26, 18:3–4)

Heart of the Story

Zipporah saved Moses's life by circumcising one of their sons to turn God's wrath from Moses.

Story Line

Zipporah was the daughter of the Midianite priest Jethro (Ruel). Jethro was a descendent of Abraham and his second wife, Keturah. Jethro worshipped God. Along with her seven sisters, Ziporrah tended her father's sheep. Daily, Jethro's daughters took the sheep to a well and filled troughs to water them. One day, other shepherds drove the girls away from the well. Moses rescued the girls and drew water for their sheep.

Jethro invited Moses to eat with him. Moses stayed with Jethro and married Zipporah. Zipporah's name means "bird," which could allude to her beauty or to a quickness of action. Moses and Zipporah had two sons. The first was named Gershom, which means "alien." The second was Eliezer, whose name means "my God is helper" (Exodus 18:3–4 NIV).

Forty years after Moses arrived in Midian, God told him to return to Egypt and free the Israelites from Egyptian slavery. When Moses started for Egypt, Zipporah, Gershom, and Eliezer were with him. On the way, God met Moses at a resting place and made Moses acutely, almost fatally, ill. Zipporah recognized that God's wrath against Moses was because he failed to circumcise a son. Immediately, Zipporah circumcised the boy. Bible readers don't know which son Zipporah circumcised; however, credible Bible scholars suggested that it was Eliezer, the second son. Possibly, Eliezer didn't understand what his mother was doing to him; but, he didn't resist her touching, even hurting, his genitals.

The Bible recorded that Zipporah touched Moses's feet with their son's foreskin. Probably, "feet" was a euphemism for genitals. She called Moses a blood-bridegroom, because she acquired him anew as a husband, i.e., she saved his life by shedding her son's blood. Zipporah's circumcision of Eliezer is the only Bible record of a mother circumcising a son.

At one point, Miriam and Aaron used Zipporah in an argument against Moses. They called Zipporah Moses's "Cushite wife," referring to either her dark complexion or her not being an Israelite. Promptly, God punished Miriam and Aaron, and showed his displeasure at their words. The Bible recorded no further Israelite criticism of Zipporah, or any discrimination against her children.

Pondering Relationships

The Bible contains scant information about Moses's wife and sons. Moses called them "Zipporah and her two sons," as if distancing himself from their presence in his life. Conceivably, Moses was embarrassed that his wife wasn't an Israelite. Alternatively, he may have been careful to keep his personal life out of the story of God's interaction with the Israelites.

Zipporah was a proactive, even independent, woman of her day. Likely, Zipporah took her sons to Jethro rather than let them live through the turmoil of the ten Egyptian plagues. She and the boys could have been used as pawns against Moses both by Egyptians, who opposed freedom for the valuable slaves, and by Israelites, who disapproved of Moses's methods.

Zipporah's death wasn't recorded. Likely, she died during the Israelite's journey in the Sinai Desert. As in most families, some of Zipporah's offspring dedicated themselves to God and the good of the Israelite nation. Others went their own way and moved far from worship of the true God.

Reflection

Why was Moses so uncommunicative about his wife and sons? With whom was Zipporah's primary relationship: God, Moses, her sons? Explain your answer.

Shunammite Woman's Son
(2 Kings 4:8–37, 8:1–6)

Heart of the Story

The Shunammite woman didn't ask Elisha for a son; however, he prayed and God gave her one. When her son died, she trusted Elisha to return him to life.

Story Line

The spectrum of events and resulting emotions seen in the Shunammite woman's life are incredible. When we first meet her, she is accepting of her motherless state. Her husband is old and hasn't fathered a child with her. She knew Israelite property laws. When her husband died, his property would go to a male relative. The male relative may, or may not, allow her to live with his family. Even if the male relative invited her to live with his family, she will no longer manage a large wealthy household.

Because of his appreciation for the Shunammite woman giving him a furnished room, Elisha tells her she will have a child in the next year. The woman's words indicate that she is overwhelmed. In her simple response to Elisha, we hear how she longs for a son. At the same time, she is afraid to get her hopes up, lest she be disappointed.

A year later, the woman had a son. Probably, she doted on him and was overcautious in her care. The son grew and one morning he went to his father in the field. There, he developed an excruciating headache. The reapers returned him to the house. Then, the mother's worst nightmare occurred—her son died. Although sobbing internally, she proceeded calmly. She took the boy's body to Elisha's room and placed him on Elisha's bed. She left the room, firmly closing the door. Servants knew they weren't to enter the prophet's room.

Telling no one of her son's death, the woman secured a donkey and a servant from her husband and rode in haste to Elisha. The distraught woman caught hold of Elisha's feet and said, "Did I ask you for a son, my lord? Didn't I tell you, 'Don't raise my hopes'?" (2 Kings 4:28 NIV). The Shunammite couldn't get the words that her son was dead past her lips;

however, Elisha surmised the problem and traveled home with her. After Elisha's prayers, God restored the boy's life.

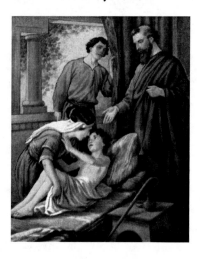

The preceding events are sufficient trauma for any one person's life; yet, there is more to come for this generous woman. On Elisha's recommendation, the Shunammite and her household left Israel because a seven-year famine was coming. They went to Philistia. After the famine, the woman and son returned to Shumen. The woman's husband wasn't mentioned; possibly, he died while the family lived in Philistia. When an Israelite father died, his son inherited the property. Sometime during the family's seven-year absence, their abandoned property was taken over by another individual or confiscated by the king.

The only way the woman and son could get their land restored was to appeal directly to the king of Israel. When they arrived in King Jehoram's (also known as Joram) audience chamber, the king listened while the Shunammite woman related how Elisha restored her son's life. Then, Jehoram gave their land back, along with the income from the land over the past seven years.

Pondering Relationships

The Bible gave the clear impression that the Shunammite woman was an initiator of action, first with her husband then for her son. Because of her, Elisha had a room in her home. Her son wasn't only born, he was restored to life. Because of her, the family survived a famine. Because of her, the king returned the family's property.

From the biblical account, we hear the Shunammite woman's emotions during each event: acceptance, disbelief, joy, anger, and determination. Particularly, she struggled to understand how God would take away her son who he gave as a demonstration of his grace.

The Bible provided no thoughts or words from the son other than an outcry when his head hurt. Possibly, he was six to seven years old when he went out to his father's fields, and thirteen to fourteen when he and his mother returned to Shumen. At that age, he was old enough to inherit his father's land and to marry. The son's witness, albeit silent, in front of the king was a testament to his life, his mother's care, and his regard for his mother.

Reflection

How would you characterize the relationship between the Shunammite woman and her son? Could this woman have been too decisive? Think about what will happen when the son marries, and his wife assumes responsibility for managing the household.

Queen Ano's Dying Son
(1 Kings 14:1–18)

Heart of the Story

When Abijah, the eldest son of King Jeroboam I, became severely ill, Queen Ano disguised herself and asked the prophet Ahijah what would happen to her son. (Note: don't be confused by the close spelling of Prince Abijah and the prophet Ahijah's names).

Story Line

The name of the first queen of the Northern Kingdom (Israel) and Jeroboam I's wife wasn't recorded in the Bible narrative; however, a footnote in The Amplified Bible (AMP) provided information about her. When Jeroboam fled to Egypt after Solomon tried to kill him, he entered Pharaoh Shishak's court. Shishak gave his sister-in-law, Ano, to Jeroboam I in marriage. Jeroboam I and Ano ruled Israel from Tirzah, a town in the tribal lands of West Manasseh. Abijah was their first son and scheduled to become ruler after Jeroboam I.

As a member of the Egyptian royal family and queen of Israel, Ano was a proud woman. She loved her eldest son, Abijah, who became very ill. Following Jeroboam I's direction, Ano disguised herself as a peasant woman and traveled twenty miles to Shiloh to ask God's prophet (Ahijah) the outcome of Abijah's illness. As a peasant, Ano traveled on a donkey with perhaps one attendant, instead of on a horse, as part of a royal cavalcade. Ano took ten loaves of bread, some cakes, and a jar of honey as an offering to the prophet. This offering was an offering from a poor woman rather than from a queen.

When Ano entered his house, Ahijah identified her and knew what she wanted. He told her that when she set foot in Tizrah, Abijah would die. There is no record that Ano pleaded with the prophet for her son's life, or that she tried to bribe him in any way. Perhaps, Ano did both; or perhaps, she recognized that the prophet's words were immutable.

Pondering Relationships

When her husband sent Queen Ano to Ahijah, Ano had no faith in the old blind prophet at Shiloh. Certainly, she didn't believe in his god; but, Ano was desperate. She wanted to know the outcome of Abijah's illness and to get help for him. Perhaps, Ano even wanted Jeroboam I to send to Egypt, the center for medical knowledge in the early Middle East, for a physician.

After leaving the prophet's home at Shiloh, Ano felt both agony and ambivalence. She wanted to be with her sick son; but, if the prophet was correct, the minute she returned to the royal city, Abijah would die. What was she to do? Perhaps as Egyptian-born royalty, Queen Ano decided to do her duty. As Jeroboam I directed, Ano returned to her husband with the prophet's words.

When Abijah died, Ano may have comforted herself with the belief that her husband's actions, not her return, caused Abijah's death. Ano was thankful she had another son, Nadab. Because she believed in Egyptian gods, not the God of the Israelites, Ano may have concluded that the prophet's words and the death of Abijah were coincidence. Whatever Ano believed, she would have mourned the death of her first-born son.

Neither King Jeroboam I nor Queen Ano worshipped God; however, perhaps, Jeroboam I worshipped God in his early years of exile in Egypt. In Hebrew, Abijah meant "my (divine) father is the Lord." Although many Egyptians consider pharaoh a god, the divine father referred to in Abijah's name was likely God. Despite his parent's beliefs and behavior, Prince Abijah had a relationship with the true God. God said that Abijah was the only one of Jeroboam I's house who had anything good in them. For this reason, God allowed Abijah to die and be buried, although all other descendants of Jeroboam I remain unburied after they died.

Reflection

Despite her noble birth and position, Queen Ano couldn't keep her son alive. How can and do Christian mothers intervene with God for the lives of their sons?

Murder of Rizpah's Sons
(2 Samuel 3:6–11, 21:1–14)

Heart of the Story

The Gibeonites killed Rizpah's sons, Armoni and Mephibosheth, and left their bodies exposed on a hill. Rizpah kept birds and wild animals off her sons' bodies for many months.

Story Line

Rizpah was King Saul's concubine. Apparently, she had some status because her father's name, Aiah, is identified in the Bible. Saul fathered Rizpah's two sons, Armoni and Mephibosheth. After Saul's death, Rizpah and her sons remained in the royal court of Ish-Bosheth, Saul's son. When Ish-Bosheth was murdered, Rizpah and sons returned to her father's family or lived with Saul's extended family in Benjamin territory.

During the early years of David's reign, Israel experienced a three-year famine associated with lack of rain. God told David that the famine was because Saul killed and almost decimated the Gibeonites. The Gibeonites were a non-Israelite people, who signed a peace treaty with Israel four hundred years earlier.

David asked the remaining Gibeonites what he could do so they would lift their curse from Israel. The Gibeonites requested seven of Saul's descendants to kill. David turned over five sons of Saul's daughter, Merab, and the two sons of Saul's concubine, Rizpah. On the first day of the barley harvest, the Gibeonites murdered and exposed the bodies of the seven men at Gibeah. Gibeah was the hometown of both the Gibeonites and Saul.

Rizpah was in a terrible position. By this time, her father was probably dead. The father of her sons, Saul, was dead. Now, her two sons were murdered. What was she to do? Who was left to provide for her?

Rizpah's next action surprised everyone. She took sackcloth and spread it out on a rock near her sons' bodies. Sackcloth is coarse, loose cloth used in mourning and for begging. Rizpah sat on the cloth. By day she kept birds and by night wild animals off her sons' bodies. Rizpah remained at the site of her sons' exposed bodies from the time they were murdered until rain poured down from heaven. This length of time could have been six to eight months or even longer. In Israel, the barley harvest starts in April, while heavy rains start in late October or November.

David learned of Rizpah's action. He gathered the bones of the seven murdered men and those of Saul and Jonathan and buried them in Saul's father's tomb at Zela, Benjamin.

Pondering Relationships

Rizpah loved her sons to the point that she exposed herself to the heat of the summer sun in Israel to protect their bodies. Smelling the decaying bodies day after day and night after night must have been excruciatingly painful. Probably, Rizpah was grateful King David gave them a consequential burial. At the same time, Rizpah must have hated David. He allowed the Gibeonites to kill her sons.

Rizpah, Armoni, and Mephibosheth were pawns in this Bible story. The Bible gives no information that the sons sinned in a way that would cause them to be murdered. Their offense was that they were sons of

Saul, who the Gibeonites justifiably blamed for killing their kin and forcing them to leave their hometown, Gibeah.

Although Rizpah's actions played a part in David's decision to bury Saul and his offspring, David made no provision for Rizpah. Unless she had brothers, or other family members, who accepted her into their household, Rizpah had an insecure future.

Reflection

Why would God want Rizpah's sons dead? Was God fair in his treatment of Rizpah?

Contemplation

The Bible never discounted the importance of a mother. "The hand that rocks the cradle, rules the world" is a common saying among Americans. It points to the centrality and power of a mother's role in a son's life up to, and including, when the son is an adult decision-maker. A mother teaches a son her own beliefs, which is why her perspectives must be congruent with God's values and commands.

In today's society, sometimes sons grow up in a motherless home. After divorce, a father may be the custodial parent; or, a mother may have died while the son is a newborn or toddler.

Pondering Mother-Son Relationships

1. What is missing in a son's life when he is motherless? How do motherless males learn to interact with women? Do you sometimes shudder when you see how boys treat mothers in television shows or in the movies? How can you offset these negative influences in your son's life?

2. Compare and contrast twenty-first century social expectation for the mother-son relationship with biblical expectations. How do the ways mothers love sons parallel how Christ loves the church, the body of all believers?

CHAPTER 4

Clans and Towns

The ancient Israelites were organized by tribes, clans, and families. Generally, Bible readers are familiar with the twelve tribes of Israel, which were descendants of Jacob's sons. Tribes consisted of many *mišpahâ*, or clans, named after a founding father, e.g., Zerahites (Douglass and Tenney, 2011). Marriage within the Hebrew clan was encouraged, and in some cases required, as with Zelophehad's daughters.

Clans were comprised of extended families. In Hebrew extended families were called *beth-ab* translated as "father's house" (Douglass and Tenney, 2011). In the extended family, all family members lived under the authority of the oldest male member. Often, the oldest male was a grandfather or great-grandfather of the youngest group member. A married daughter was counted in her husband's family. The clan and extended family protected members and maintained ancestry records. These records were transcribed and handed down from generation to generation, as the genealogy of Christ in Matthew.

When the Israelites entered the Promised Land, extended families formed villages and later towns for protection. Usually, villages and towns formed around agriculture. Ancient farmers didn't work their own farms in the way early American settlers had farmsteads. Instead, members worked the land together for the extended family. Livestock and crops were an enticement to wandering tribes, e.g., Midianites. Farmers entered the village or town at night for their own safety and to protect their families. At times, farmers took their most valuable livestock with them inside the village or town.

The main difference between a village and town was the size and number of extended families who lived there. Towns had more people living in them and they had a town wall. Walls were as thick as thirty feet. The town had a gate or gates that were closed at night and on the Sabbath. Men, on the wall or in a lookout tower, watched for maundering tribes and attackers.

Another feature of a town was a widened area inside the town gate. This widened area was a place for community life and social interaction. Here, the town's people held assemblies, exchanged news, transacted business, and administered justice. When no Israelite invited a stranger to his home, he remained overnight in this area.

In chapter 4, the stories of six groups are told. Three were clans, named after their clan founder. None of the clans were Israelites; Israelite people called them "aliens." The Gibeonites lived in Canaan when the Israelites arrived there. Most likely Kenites and Racabites came into the Promised Land with the Israelites. God commanded Israelites to not mistreat aliens who lived with them in the Promised Land. Instead, Israelites should love aliens as they loved themselves. When he gave this commandment, God reasoned that the Israelites were once aliens in Egypt.

Three stories are about men who lived in designated towns. They have the name of their town, e.g., the townsmen of Jabesh Gilead, Succoth, and Lystra. The men of Jabesh Gilead and Succoth were Israelites, who lived east of the Jordan River. Lystra was a New Testament town in Asia Minor. Lystra exposes the effect of different cultural groups living in the same area. Stories encompass:

- The Gibeonites
- The Kenites
- The Recabites
- Elders of Succoth
- Men of Jabesh Gilead
- New Testament Lystrans

The Gibeonites
(Joshua 9, 10:1–10; 2 Samuel 21:1–6)

Heart of the Story

The Gibeonites obtained a peace treaty with the Israelites using deception. Because the Israelites swore their oath before God, there was no end point for it.

Story Line

God commanded the Israelites to kill all Canaanite inhabitants when they entered the Promised Land. Some Canaan kings joined together to battle the Israelites. The men of Gibeah were an exception. The Gibeonites determined to sign a peace treaty with the Israelites. Their leaders arrived at the Israelite camp at Gilgal in worn clothes and shoes and carried moldy, dry provisions and cracked wineskins. They claimed to have traveled a long distance to obtain a peace treaty with the Israelites, whom they feared. Without consulting God, Joshua and the tribal leaders agreed to a treaty with the Gibeonites and swore to it before God.

Three days later, the Israelites learned that the Gibeonites were their neighbors. The Israelites went to the town of Gibeah. They told the Gibeonites that they would honor the treaty; however, in the future, the Gibeonites had to cut wood and carry water for the Israelite community and the Tabernacle.

Because the Gibeonites had a treaty with the Israelites, five Amorite kings moved their armies to attack Gibeah. The Gibeonites sent a message to the Israelites, begging for help. Joshua and his men completed a twenty-mile, all-night march from Gilgal to Gibeah. They took the Amorite army by surprise and routed them. Gibeah was saved.

For the next four hundred years, the Bible provided little information on the Gibeonites. Apparently, they fulfilled their duties as outlined in the treaty. While Saul was king, he violated the Israelite-Gibeonite treaty by killing many Gibeonites. Those not killed were driven from their homes and no longer considered part of Israel. The reasons for King Saul's actions aren't completely clear. Perhaps, Saul felt a sense of nationalism and determined to rid his country of aliens living in their midst.

Alternatively, Saul's home was Gibeah; he didn't want a large non-Israelite clan living in his hometown.

During David's reign there was a three-year famine. When David asked God the reason for it, God told him it was because of Saul's bloody attack on the Gibeonites. David met with the remaining Gibeonites. He asked them what he could do to appease their anger so they would remove their curse from Israel. The Gibeonites weren't interested in material compensation. They wanted the lives of seven of Saul's descendants. David acceded to the Gibeonite's request. He handed over five sons of Saul's daughter Merab and two sons of Saul's concubine. The Gibeonites killed all seven men and left their bodies exposed.

Pondering Relationships

God's plan was for the Israelites to kill all Canaanites who lived in the land. Had Joshua sought God's will when the Gibeonites came to the Israelite camp, God would have shown him the Gibeonite's subterfuge. Why did Joshua neglect God's counsel? Was he puffed-up over past victories? Did Joshua believe he understood what God wanted, therefore, could get on with the process of conquering Canaan? Did Joshua simply forget to ask God about such a simple matter? Whatever Joshua's motivation, he was taken in by the Gibeonites and committed the Israelites to a course of action outside God's guidelines.

When King David asked God the reason for the Israelite famine, he expected God to identify a current national sin. David forgot that Joshua signed a peace treaty with the Gibeonites, when the Israelites first entered the Promised Land 450 years earlier. Although time dulled the Israelite's memory of their treaty with the Gibeonites, it didn't dull God's memory. God expected King Saul to honor the Israelite-Gibeonite treaty. Further, he expected the Israelites to treat resident aliens like they treated their own people.

Reflection

Does God really expect Christians to keep all promises made to others? Are we accountable to God for promises made by our ancestors?

The Kenites
(Genesis 15:18–19; Numbers 10:29–32, 24:22–23; Judges 1:16, 4:11–24; 1 Samuel 27:10, 30:29)

Heart of the Story

The Kenites were a non-Israelite, loosely knit people. Some of their members aligned themselves with Israel. The Israelites allowed the allied Kenites to live in their lands and share in God's bounty.

Story Line

The Kenites were a nomadic people, who were both condemned and praised in the Bible. The first time they were mentioned, God made a covenant with Abram, giving him the land from the Nile River to the Euphrates River. The Kenites lived in this area. The second time the Kenites are mentioned, the Israelites were making their final march north from the Sinai Peninsula to Jericho. The Moabite king hired a well-known seer, Balaam, to prophesy against the Israelites. Balaam saw Kenites among the Moab coalition. He prophesied that although the Kenites made their home in rocky areas and felt secure, Asshur (Assyria) would take them captive.

In contrast to these questionable views, some Kenites were strong supporters of the Israelites. Jethro, Moses's father-in-law, was a Kenite, as was his son Hobab. After building the Tabernacle, the Israelites moved northward toward the Promised Land. Moses implored Hobab to be their scout. Hobab was familiar with the land the Israelites would pass through. He knew the best places to camp and where water could be found in these desert areas. Moses promised that if Hobab went with them, the Israelites would share with him whatever the Lord gave them. Hobab and his family agreed to travel with the Israelites. The Bible recorded that descendants of Jethro traveled with Judah and lived with them in the Negev Desert near Arad.

About two hunred years after the Israelites entered the Promised Land, a Kenite named Heber left the Arad area and moved to the hill country of Naphtali. The Kenites were metal workers. Heber worked for King Jabin of Hazor and helped build the nine hundred chariots in Jabin's army. With the assistance of these chariots, Sisera, Jabin's war commander, cruelly oppressed the Israelites for twenty years.

God raised the judge, Deborah, to free the Israelites. When the Israelite army routed Sisera's army, he fled to Heber's camp. Heber wasn't home. His wife, Jael, invited Sisera to rest in her tent. There, Sisera drank milk and fell into an exhausted sleep. Jael killed Sisera by driving a tent peg through his temple.

Pondering Relationships

The Israelites kept Moses's promise of peace and mutual aid to the Kenites. Early in King Saul's reign, God ordered him to destroy the Amalekites. Both the Amalekites and Kenites lived in the southern Negev Desert. King Saul warned the Kenites to leave the area, so they weren't mistakenly killed along with the Amalekites. The reason Saul gave for sparing the Kenites was that they showed kindness to the Israelites when they came out of Egypt.

When David was on the run from King Saul, he became a Philistine vassal. David told the Philistines that he was attacking Judah and the Kenites in southern Israel. In reality, David raided Judah's enemies and sent gifts from his spoils to both Judah and the Kenites. David saw the Kenites as allies of Judah.

Reflection

Both the Gibeonites and Kenites were aliens who lived in Israel. What did they do to earn disparate treatment from King Saul?

The Recabites
(Jeremiah 35; 2 Kings 10:15–17)

Heart of the Story

The Recabites lived by standards set by their ancestor Jonadab; yet Judah ignored the commandments set by their God.

Story Line

The Recabites were a non-Jewish people, closely aligned with the Israelites. They were nomadic or seminomadic. Most scholars believe they were kinsmen of the Kenites and entered the Promised Land with the Israelites. When the Bible first mentioned the Recabites, they lived in the Northern Kingdom (Israel). Their leader, Jonadab (also known as Jehonadab), was head of a conservative movement that believed in God. Vehemently, he opposed the worship of Baal.

Shortly after King Jehu destroyed the house of King Ahab and Queen Jezebel, Jonadab went out to meet him. After Jonadab assured King Jehu of his support, Jehu took him into his chariot. Public association with Jonadab added to Jehu's status among the rural population of Israel and provided support for Jehu's plan to demolish Baal's temples and kill Baal's priests.

For the next 250 years, the Bible is silent about the Recabites. A Jeremiah-Recabite interaction took place during the reign of King Jehoiakim (609–598 BC), when Judah was overran by the Babylonians. At that time, the Recabites moved inside the Jerusalem walls to escape the marauding armies.

The Lord told Jeremiah to gather the Recab family into a side room of the temple and serve them wine. Following God's direction, Jeremiah brought Jaazaniah, his brothers, and sons into the temple. Jeremiah set wine before the Recabites and told them to drink. The Recabites declined the wine. They explain that their ancestor, Jonadab, told them to never drink wine, plant vineyards, or sow seeds. They were to live in tents rather than build houses. If they followed Jonadab's directions, they would live a long time in the land.

Pondering Relationships

The Recabite's commitment to Jonadab's command provided God with a powerful object lesson for Judah and Jerusalem. Although the Recabites remained true to their ancestor's instructions, Judah didn't remain true to God's instructions. We can almost see God shaking his head, marveling: if the non-Israelite Recabites carried out their ancestor's directions, why did Judah refuse to carry out the commands of a caring God who gave them the land and its abundance?

Because the people of Judah ignored God when he called and spoke to them God planned to bring on Judah every disaster, i.e., famine, pestilence, and death, pronounced against them by God's prophets. In contrast to Judah, the future for the Recabites was secure. Because they obeyed their ancestor, the clan would always have a man to serve God. The Jewish Mishnah claimed that the Recabites were given special duties to perform in the second Jerusalem temple, built after the Babylonian exile (Metzger and Coogan, 2004).

When we visited Petra, Jordan, we had a long conversation with our camel driver. He lived in a Bedouin village near Petra. He introduced us to his cousin, whom he called a brother in the way of extended families. The brother's family lived in tents—large, beautiful tents—near Petra.

These Bedouins are seminomads even today. Like the Racabites, the young men honored their ancestors and heritage. With love and respect, the camel driver spoke of his father, who was aging and becoming hard of hearing. Similar to the Racabites, the young men knew the foundation of their beliefs and their place in the world.

Reflection

God wanted the nation of Judah to show him the same honor that the Racabites showed Jonadab. How do we honor or dishonor our relationship with cousins, grandparents, or other extended family members? How do we honor or dishonor our relationship with God?

Elders of Succoth
(Judges 8:4–17)

Heart of the Story

When Gideon pursued the Midianite army, Succoth officials refused to give his army food. After defeating the Midian army, Gideon punished the town elders.

Story Line

Because the Israelites started to worship Canaanite gods, God allowed the Midianites to oppress them for seven years. They killed the Israelite's livestock and ruined their crops. The Israelites were reduced to living in mountain clefts, caves, and strongholds. Eventually, the Israelites called out to God, who raised Gideon to free them.

Gideon was from Manasseh, the only Israelite tribe that had land on both sides of the Jordan River. Gideon's home was west of the Hordan River. With three hundred Israelite men, Gideon overcame the main Midianite army; however, ten thousand Midianites escaped across the Jordan River. Pursuing them, Gideon and his men came to Succoth, a town about four miles east of the Jordan River in the tribal lands of Gad.

Manasseh and Gad tribesmen knew each other. Half of Manasseh's tribal lands bordered Gad on the north. The fordable Jordan River separated the two tribes on Gad's west. The Succoth elders knew how viciously the Midianites oppressed the central and northern Israelite tribes. Probably, they knew about Gideon's roust of the Midianites in the Jezreel Valley. Despite the lack of telephone and internet, news traveled fast in the ancient world.

Gideon asked the Succoth officials for bread for his weary army. Gideon had every reason to expect encouragement and support from the town. The twelve tribes had agreed that in times of national danger, they would fight to protect each other. The Succoth official's refusal to feed Gideon's army was shocking! Even more so was their insolent taunt that Gideon hadn't yet captured or killed the Midianite chiefs. So why should they aid him?

Because Gideon wanted to pursue the Midianites, he took no immediate action against the Succoth officials; however, he promised to return and punish them. After leaving Succoth, Gideon defeated the Midianites and captured two of their kings, Zebah and Zalmunna. Gideon and his men returned to the Succoth area. They caught a young man of Succoth who wrote down the names of the seventy-seven Succoth officials.

Pondering Relationship

When Gideon entered Succoth, he showed the captured Midian kings to the town officials and reminded them of their taunting words. Then, Gideon and his army used thorns and briers to punish the town officials. In today's world, thorns and briers are rarely used for punishment; however, in the ancient world, they were a common method of punishment. Thorns and briers were placed on a man's naked body and pressed down by a heavy wooden sleigh. Sleighs (sledges) were dragged back and forth over the individual's body, so thorns and brier spines dug deep into and tore the skin. Given the Succoth officials very public and insolent refusal to assist Gideon's hungry army, soldiers were enthusiastic in their punishment.

The reason that the Succoth officials refused aid to Gideon and his army was because they feared reprisal from the Midianites. Fear is a normal reaction to a real threat; but, Succoth's fear came with foreswearing of the promise of common support for their Israelite brothers. I wonder if Gideon would have been as angry if the Succoth officials were open and honest. They could have said something like, "We want to aid you; but, are afraid that if you don't win the battle, we will be attacked and killed by the Midianites." True, they would have lost face; but, they would have been less offensive to Gideon's troops. Jubilant from their victory against the Midianites, Gideon's army may have forgotten or forgiven the town's taunts.

Reflection

Have you ever refused to help a fellow Christian in need? How did your actions hurt that person? How did your actions hurt you?

Men of Jabesh Gilead
(Judges 20; 1 Samuel 11;
2 Samuel 2:4–8, 21:10–14)

Heart of the Story

The men from Jabesh Gilead secretly stole the bones of King Saul and his sons from Beth Shan where the Philistines hung them.

Story Line

Jabesh Gilead was east of the Jordan River in the tribal lands of northern Gad. The men of Jabesh Gilead were independent thinkers. Early in Promised Land history, they refused to adhere to the Israelite standard for unified, mutual aid. The Jabesh Gilead men didn't join the Israelite's retaliation against the Benjaminites over a murdered concubine. The tribes of Gad and Benjamin were geographically, and possibly emotionally, aligned. When the Israelites journeyed in the wilderness, Benjamin and Gad marched next to each other and camped beside each other. In the Promised Land, Benjamin was west of Gad across the Jordan River.

Because the men of Jabesh Gilead didn't join the battle against Benjamin, the Israelites killed all who were in the town, except four hundred virgins. These women were given to the Benjaminites to rebuild their tribe.

Sometime later, an Ammonite king, Nahash, besieged Jabesh Gilead. Townsmen asked Nahash for terms of surrender. King Nahash said he would make a treaty with them only if townsmen allowed him to gouge out their right eye. Gouging out the right eye would destroy the men's military capability, particularly the archers. The elders of Jabesh Gilead asked Nahash for time to contact their Israelite brothers. If Israelites didn't rescue them in seven days, they would accept Nahash's surrender terms. Given their history of refusing to stand with the Israelites over the matter of the murdered concubine, neither the Ammonites nor the Jabesh Gilead men expected Israelites to come to their aid.

One town that Jabesh Gilead appealed for aid was Gibeah in Benjamin. The newly crowned King Saul's home was Gibeah. When Saul heard the plight of Jabesh Gilead, the spirit of God came upon him. Saul rallied 330,000 soldiers and slaughtered the Ammonites.

Pondering Relationships

Following Saul's rescue, the Jabesh Gilead men developed an intense loyalty to him. This loyalty was so deep-seated that they entered a fortified Philistine city at night and took the bodies of Saul and his sons from the town wall. The Bible used the word *valiant* to describe the actions by the men of Jabesh Gilead. Valiant is the same word that was used to describe Saul's warriors, whose hearts God touched.

Possibly, the men of Jabesh Gilead believed the Philistines wouldn't know who took Saul's body. More probably, they knew the Philistines would learn they had Saul's bones, but they didn't care. Saul was their king. He brought them aid against the Ammonites, when no other Israelite city or tribe stepped forward. King Saul preserved their ability to act as warriors in the paramilitary environment where they lived.

The men of Jabesh Gilead didn't retrieve Saul's body because they were loyal to the Israelite monarchy. If believing in the monarchy motivated their retrieval of Saul's body, they would have accepted, rather than ignored, King David's request for support. They didn't follow Saul because they believed that a king would protect them from their enemies, as many Israelites believed. No, their loyalty and actions were directed toward Saul, the man.

After burying Saul, the men of Jabesh Gilead mourned his death for seven days. Seven days is the traditional amount of time that an Israelite mourned the death of a first degree relative, i.e., father, wife, child.

Can you imagine your hometown acting in one accord? That's what the Bible recorded as happening in Jabesh Gilead; however, I wouldn't be surprised, if certain Jabesh Gilead townsmen had doubts. Surely, some thought that creeping into a mighty Philistine town at night to recover Saul's body was a really bad idea. They could be killed for retrieving an already dead body. Nonetheless, in extended families, male elders were final decision-makers for the family group. The male elders in Jabesh Gilead were men whom Saul rescued. To them, Saul wasn't only their king; he was family.

Reflection

Christians often speak of their church family. Do you consider members of your church as family? Ponder your loyalty to church members. What are the limits of your loyalty? Are only selected church members, i.e., ones you know best, family or are all family?

New Testament Lystrans
(Acts 14:7–20)

Heart of the Story

Paul and Barnabas visited Lystra on his first missionary journey. After hailing the missionaries as gods, townsmen attempted to kill them.

Story Line

Lystra was built on the southern edge of the fertile Lycaonia plain. Behind Lystra rose the gigantic Taurus Mountains. In 6 BC, Augustus Caesar made Lystra a Roman colony and stationed there the Roman garrison for southern Galatia. Augustus hoped to keep the plunder and blackmail of the wild mountaineers in check and open the area for peaceful settlement.

Lystra was a multicultural town. It was home to soldiers who retired from Roman legions. The military and former military were the aristocracy of Lystra. Latin was the official language in the town. Some of the Lystran culture was Greek. A temple to Zeus was located near the town entrance. Local legend claimed that the Greek chief god, Zeus, visited the area, but was recognized only by a pious couple. Although some Jews lived in Lystra, the number was small. Lystra didn't have a Jewish synagogue. Among themselves, Lystrans spoke their native tongue, Lycaonian.

Paul visited Lystra on his first missionary journey, probably in AD 49. He preached the good news of Christ to the townspeople. Soon after his arrival, Paul healed a crippled man who was unable to walk from birth. When the Lystrans saw the man walking, they identified Barnabas as Zeus, the chief Greek god. They identified Paul as Hermes, the Greek messenger of the gods, because he did most of the speaking. The priests from Zeus's temple brought garlands for each apostle's neck and planned to sacrifice bulls in their honor. They were determined not to neglect their god's visit a second time.

When Paul and Barnabas understood what was happening, they tore their clothes. They dashed among the people, saying they were men just like the Lystrans. They assured the people that God wanted them to turn from idol worship and worship him, the living God. With difficulty,

Paul and Barnabas were able to prevent the townspeople from offering sacrifices to them.

Then, Jews from Antioch and Iconium came to Lystra. These Jews poisoned the Lystran's minds against Paul and Barnabas. The result was that Lystrans stoned Paul. Thinking he was dead, they dragged Paul outside the town. When the disciples gathered around Paul, he stood up and walked back into Lystra. The next day Paul and Barnabas left Lystra.

Pondering Relationship

Families, towns, clans, and nations often react to embarrassment and shame by striking out. Because they can't take rage out on themselves, they take it out on others. The Lystrans were embarrassed when they learned Paul and Barnabas told the same story in Antioch and Iconium. Both towns were larger and more polished than Lystra. In neither place did townspeople characterize Paul and Barnabas as gods. In fact, they ran them out of town!

The priests of the Temple of Zeus were furious. They were ready to worship the missionaries as Zeus and Hermes, only to learn that the missionaries wanted to replace Zeus worship with worship of some unknown god, called Christ. Their status as priests of Zeus was threatened by Paul and Barnabas's message. How could they have believed that the king of the Greek gods came to visit tiny Lystra in the outback of the Roman Empire?

Notice the difference between the composition of towns in Old and New Testament times. Lystra was a multicultural town made up of retired Roman legionnaires, active duty Roman soldiers, Greeks, Jews, and native Lycaonians. When a town grows beyond a single culture, often townspeople don't work together under a single leader. Residents don't all have the same point of view. Diverse groups see events from their own perspective. Factions and dissensions often develop when individuals of different cultures live in the same area.

Reflection

How did Lystra, being a multicultural town, impact the Lystran's relationship with the missionaries? Was it better for the Lystrans to take their anger out on Paul rather than on new Christian church members?

Contemplation

"The thing most needed in the American home today is the family" is an anonymous quote that is being heard more and more in the twenty-first century. In ancient Israel, family had blood ties. Today, family encompasses emotional ties as much as genetic ties.

Just as the Kenites had disparate members, extended families today are composed of disparate members. They believe differently and act differently. Being from a Christian family doesn't ensure a right relationship with God. Each individual must make a personal decision to follow God.

Americans believe that they can and should make their own decisions about what to do and not to do. Often, they don't ask extended family members for advice. This perspective could be a help or a hindrance to wise personal decision-making.

Pondering Extended Family Relationships

1. Think and discuss your responsibility to extended family members, e.g., aunts, cousins, grandparents. Do you have any relatives that you want to be proactive in helping?

2. Almost every American town or city contains individuals from many cultures. Many have religious beliefs very different from Christian beliefs. With the exception of Paul, the Lystrans didn't attack Christians when they were a minority group in Lystra. Does that example mean that where Christians are a majority, they should be tolerant of the faith of others?

CHAPTER 5

Masters and Slaves/Servants

In ancient cultures, slavery was rampant, particularly in the Roman Empire. Among the Israelites, slaves were acquired through war, purchase, and gifts. If a thief had no money to pay for a stolen object, he became a slave until the cost was paid. Individuals living in poverty could sell themselves as slaves. Poor fathers sometimes sold their children into slavery.

Mosaic law governed the treatment of slaves. Israelite slave laws demanded a more humane treatment of slaves than in other nations. Most Israelite slave laws focused on how to treat fellow Israelites who became slaves.

Israelites who became slaves of other Israelites weren't personal property. They functioned more like bond or indentured servants. After six years, Israelites must free male Israelite slaves. Female slaves didn't have to be freed after six years; however, their family could buy them back at any time. An Israelite owner couldn't sell a female slave to foreigners. If the owner's son married a female slave, she was no longer a slave. She became a daughter in the family.

An Israelite man who married a slave couldn't neglect her even if he took another wife. The rights of the slave-wife included food, clothing, and sexual intimacy. If the owner failed to provide these, the slave-wife was free to leave him without making restitution.

Israelite slaveholders couldn't kill or maim slaves or bond servants. When an Israelite beat a slave/servant and the slave died, the owner was punished. If a slaveholder hit a male or female slave in the face and knocked a tooth out, or in the eye and blindness resulted, the owner had to set the slave free.

Early Christians owned slaves and had long-term servants. Writing to the Ephesian church, Paul reminded slave owners not to threaten their slaves. Instead, slave owners should remember that they have a master in heaven who they will answer to. Paul warned slave owners that God has no favorites, whether slave or free.

In the New Testament, slaves served in Christian and non-Christian households. In several letters, Paul provided guidelines for the way slaves/ servants should act. They should obey their earthly masters with respect and fear and serve them with sincerity as they served Christ. Slaves/serv- ants should work with enthusiasm, knowing that they were working for God, not for their masters. These guidelines applied to slaves/servants who served kind and reasonably good masters and those with inconsider- ate, cruel masters. God is pleased when slaves/servants patiently endure unfair treatment.

This chapter contains the stories of six master-slave/servant dyads. With the exception of the story of Hegai, the six stories were set in either an Israelite or Christian environment. These servants/slaves impacted Israelite history, and through it, the Christian church. Some slaves were valued, some were neglected. One had the audacity to run away from his master. With the exception of Gehazi and, initially, Onesimus, the slaves/ servants were hero/heroines. They respectfully obeyed their masters and served them sincerely, even enthusiastically. I have sequenced these sto- ries from the most to least optimal. As always, please decide if you agree or you believe they should be resequenced. The six relationships are:

- Naaman's valued slaves/servants

- Hegai, eunuch over the harem

- Rhoda, excitable servant

- Onesimus, slave and son

- Bilhah and Zilpah, slaves, servants, or wives?

- Gehazi, greedy servant

Naaman's Valued Slaves/Servants
(2 Kings 5:1–19)

Heart of the Story

Naaman was one of the most powerful men in the Near East. Through the intervention of two of his slaves/servants, Naaman was cured from leprosy.

Story Line

Naaman was a valiant soldier and commander of the Aram army. The Aram king, Ben-Hadad, credited Aram's military victories to Commander Naaman. Unfortunately, Naaman had a skin disease that the Bible labeled leprosy, a disfiguring and disabling infection.

An Israelite girl was captured during an Aram raid into Israel territory. Naaman took her to serve his wife. Either the girl knew Elisha directly or knew his reputation as a prophet and healer. She told her mistress that Elisha could cure Naaman. Naaman's wife valued the girl's opinion and recounted the girl's words to her husband.

Desperate to be healed, Naaman took the information to King Ben-Hadad. Immediately, Ben-Hadad encouraged Naaman to go to Israel and see the prophet. He wrote an introductory letter to Joram (also known as Jehoram), king of Israel and expressed confidence that Naaman would be healed.

When Naaman's caravan arrived in Samaria, King Joram was flabbergasted both by the letter and by the presence of Naaman. As he pondered what to do, Joram received a message from the prophet Elisha. Elisha told Joram to send Naaman to him. Joram must have sighed with relief. Perhaps, he could blame Elisha for not curing Naaman and get out of this situation without going to war with Aram.

By this point, Naaman may have considered that he was getting the run around; however, he and his entourage left the Israelite royal court and traveled to Elisha's home on Mount Carmel. Rudely, Elisha didn't invite the powerful commander inside his home for a meal or even go out to meet him. Instead, Elisha sent a message to Naaman—probably through his servant Gehazi—telling him to wash himself seven times in the Jordan River. Naaman was beyond angry by Elisha's actions. He fumed that:

- Elisha didn't come out of his home to greet him.

- Elisha didn't stand in front of him and call on God or wave his hand over Naaman's infectious site.

- What did Elisha mean, wash in the Jordan River? If all it took to cure Naaman was washing seven times in a river, he could wash in a Damascus river, better than any water in Israel.

Naaman left Elisha's home in a rage. Soon afterward, Naaman's servants approached him, even knowing the war commander was furious. The servants had a close relationship with Naaman. They addressed Naaman, as "my father." Then, the servants suggested that if Elisha required some great task, Naaman would do it. Wouldn't Naaman complete the simple task of washing seven times in the Jordan River? In response, Naaman went to the Jordan and washed seven times. His flesh was restored and became clean like that of a young boy.

Pondering Relationships

Naaman and his wife must have been benevolent master and mistress. Servants cared about their master's health and were proactive in trying to rid Naaman of leprosy. The young slave girl was comfortable enough with her mistress to share her belief that an Israelite prophet could cure Naaman. Neither master nor mistress was so proud that they refused to take advice from a slave or servants.

Naaman's male servants considered it safe to suggest an action that a furious Naaman rejected earlier. For servants to address a powerful war commander as "father" was exceptional. They must have been with Naaman a long time and had a close relationship with him. The Bible recorded the exploits of many war commanders, e.g., Sisera, Joab, Abner, and Nebuzaradan, two of which were Israelites. Nowhere is there a tender conversation between a master and servants, similar to that between Naaman and his servant. Nowhere else in the Bible do we read that servants called a master "father."

Reflection

Naaman was a pagan who worshipped Rimmon, the Aram nature god. Naaman followed no commandments from God that told him how to treat servants. Why did he treat his servants, including one who was from an enemy country, considerately?

Hegai, Eunuch Over the Harem
(Esther 2:1–18)

Heart of the Story

Esther trusted Hegai to give her good advice. Hegai facilitated Esther's rise to the position of queen of Persia.

Story Line

Hegai was a eunuch, a castrated male, in charge of the virgin's harem in the Persian king's court at Susa. Shortly after Xerxes I (also named Ahasuerus) became king, he divorced his wife, Vashti. Then, he went to war. When he returned home after an unsuccessful campaign against the Greeks, Xerxes I began to think about Vashti. To prevent a possible reconciliation, Xerxes I's personal attendants proposed that the most beautiful young virgins in the Persian Empire be brought to Susa. The virgins would be placed under Hegai's care. After twelve months of beauty treatments—six months with oil of myrrh and six months with perfume and cosmetics—each virgin would spend a night with King Xerxes I. From the virgins, Xerxes I would choose the next queen of Persia. The Jewish historian Josephus wrote that four hundred virgins were assembled in the harem (Whiston, 1987).

The Persian Empire stretched from India to Ethiopia. Searching for beautiful virgins in all 127 provinces and bringing them to Susa took months, possibly years. Virgins who lived in Susa were taken to the Susa harem first. One virgin was a Jewish girl named Esther. Esther's parents were dead. She was reared by a caring older cousin, Mordecai. Esther was lovely to look at and had a beautiful figure and character.

Esther won Hegai's favor. He treated her differently from other virgins in four ways. First, Hegai started Esther's year of beauty treatments immediately, thus expedited her introduction to King Xerxes I. Second, Hegai gave Esther special food. Third, he assigned her seven maids. Fourth, Hegai moved Esther and her maids into the best suite of rooms in the harem. During her year-long preparation, Esther won the favor of everyone who saw her.

On the night a virgin went to the king, she could take anything with her that she desired. Possibly, some virgins took cosmetics and perfume; others may have taken beautiful nightgowns and jewelry. Some may have taken the Persian equivalent of a toothbrush and mouthwash. The Bible doesn't identify what Esther took with her to King Xerxes I's chamber. We are told only that Esther took what Hegai recommended. Esther concluded that Hegai knew what appealed to King Xerxes I. She trusted Hegai to provide her with the best advice available. The outcome of the night Esther spent with King Xerxes I was that Esther became queen of Persia.

Pondering Relationships

King Xerxes I had many eunuchs in the royal court. His seven personal attendants were eunuchs, as were the keepers of the king's harem of virgins and harem of concubines. In Egypt, Assyria, and throughout the Persian Empire, eunuchs were valued servants/slaves. About five hundred boys were castrated every year to serve Persian royalty and the very wealthy in the Empire.

Hegai, who met the most exquisite virgins in the Persian Empire, saw that Esther was exceptional. He gave Esther unmerited preferential treatment that leaves us wondering about his motivation. Perhaps, Hegai selfishly hoped that if Esther became queen, she would give him special favors. Maybe, Hegai saw a lovely girl whose potential he didn't want to see wasted in the harem of concubines. Conceivably, Hegai was a Jew. When he saw Mordecai walk outside the harem each day to check on Esther, he recognized Mordecai's nationality; thus, Hegai promoted Esther.

Despite these possible reasons for Hegai's favoritism toward Esther, the more reasonable explanation is that God ordained Hegai's actions on Esther's behalf. Whatever Hegai's nationality or sexuality, God has ultimate control of each life on earth. He can harden or soften a heart toward an individual, as he softened Hegai's heart toward Esther. Without Hegai, Esther may not have been in a position to later save Jewish lives in the Persian Empire.

Reflection

God uses unlikely individuals to further his purpose and kingdom. Like me, do you normally search for temporal reasons and meanings for events rather than acknowledge God's sovereignty? Do you think Hegai knew and had a relationship with God?

Rhoda, Excitable Servant
(Acts 12:13–16)

Heart of the Story

After an angel freed Peter from prison, he went to Mary's house, where Christians were assembled. When Rhoda heard Peter's voice, she was so excited that she forgot to let him inside the door.

Story Line

About ten years after the death of Christ, King Herod Agrippa I had the apostle James beheaded and put Peter in prison. Agrippa I planned on putting Peter on trial. The night before the public trial, an angel appeared in Peter's cell. Without disturbing the guards, the angel woke Peter. The chains fell off Peter's hands. The angel led Peter out of prison. On the street, the angel left Peter. Then, it dawned on Peter that he wasn't having a dream; he was really free! Peter's first thought was to go to Mary's house.

Mary was the mother of John Mark, and an early believer in Christ. Her home was a gathering place for the fledgling church. Members were there that night, praying for Peter's release. Potentially, they were holding an all-night prayer meeting. Losing another church leader, particularly one of Peter's stature, would devastate the young church.

Mary's home was fairly spacious. The house had an outer courtyard door, which faced the street. The door was without a window or peephole. It was only opened when someone inside the home recognized a knocker's voice. When Peter knocked on the outer door, Rhoda answered the door. More than likely, she asked, "Who's there?" Rhoda wasn't about to open the door to just anyone in the middle of the night. When Peter identified himself, Rhoda recognized his voice. In her joy, Rhoda forgot to open the door. Instead she ran back to the prayer group and said, "Peter is at the door" (Acts 12:14 NIV).

Although the church was praying for Peter's release, they told her, "You're out of your mind" (Acts 12:15 NIV). When Rhoda insisted that Peter was at the door, the members declared that it wasn't Peter, but his angel. The early church believed that everyone had a personal angel who ministered to them (Hebrews 1:14). Peter kept knocking on the outer door. Eventually, someone opened it. When the church members saw Peter, they were astonished and delighted.

Pondering Relationships

Rhoda was a servant in Mary's household. She was called a girl; therefore, she was about ten years old. Because she was assigned to open the outer house door, she was conscientious and sensible. Rhoda could discern who to let in and who to contact the owner before admitting.

Although young and lacking in worldly experience, Rhoda believed that God answered prayers. She had no problem believing that Peter, not his ministering angel, was at the door. She persisted in telling those assembled that Peter was here.

Rhoda knew Peter's voice. In the early church, slaves and/or servants worshiped with owners and freemen and women. Likely, Rhoda heard Peter preach and pray. Rhoda was so excited that Peter was free that she wanted everyone in Mary's house to know immediately. Peter understood that it was Rhoda's joy that caused her to leave him exposed outside the door. In his own way, Peter was just as excited and stunned by his release.

Reflection

Often, children believe in the outcome of prayer, while adults spend time pondering reasons why God doesn't answer prayers. What are specific ways to become more like Rhoda in your relationship with God and in your prayer life?

Onesimus, Slave and Son (Philemon)

Heart of the Story

Paul called a runaway slave his son and begged his owner to treat him as a Christian brother.

Story Line

Onesimus was a runaway slave who belonged to Philemon, a wealthy Christian who lived in Colossae. The story of Onesimus is told in a letter from Paul to Philemon. Paul never visited Colossae, but on his third missionary journey, Paul spent several years in Ephesus. There, Paul met Philemon, who he led to saving belief in Christ. The Bible is silent on whether or not Paul encountered Onesimus in Ephesus.

Assuredly, Onesimus knew about Paul and the new Christian faith his owner embraced.

Paul was in Rome under house arrest (AD 59–61/62) when Onesimus ran from Philemon. Apparently, Onesimus stole money or valuables, which he used to pay for passage on a ship bound for Rome. Rome was a frequent destination of runaway slaves. In a population of one million people, it was easy to remain hidden; however, Onesimus didn't remain hidden from his destiny.

In Rome, Onesimus heard Paul, or another missionary, preach. He converted to Christianity. Soon, Onesimus began to help Paul with his ministry. Onesimus and Paul became so close that Paul described himself as Onesimus's father and Onesimus as his child. Although they wanted to stay together, both agreed that Philemon had a prior claim on Onesimus. Onesimus must make restitution to Philemon. Onesimus returned to Philemon in Colossae. With him, Onesimus took a personal letter from Paul, begging Philemon to be lenient toward his runaway slave.

Pondering Relationships

In the Roman Empire, slaves were property. The master of a runaway slave could treat the slave anyway he desired. Normal procedure was for owners to brand captured slaves on the forehead, maim them, or force them to fight wild beasts in a Roman arena. Being a Christian, Philemon wouldn't have subjected Onesimus to such extreme punishment; however, he would have punished Onesimus, e.g., flogging, poor food and housing, or the worst jobs.

Paul didn't deny or negate the seriousness of Onesimus's action when he ran from Philemon; yet, Paul saw the hand of God in Onesimus's flight. Now, Philemon will have Onesimus back, no longer as a slave, but as a dear brother. Tactfully, Paul asked Philemon to forego punishment of Onesimus. Paul used a lighthearted play on Onesimus's name in the request. The name Onesimus meant "useful" or "profitable." When Onesimus ran away from Philemon, he was "useless." Now as a Christian brother, Onesimus is "useful," both to Paul and to Philemon. Paul offered to reimburse Philemon for any money or valuables that his son stole from Philemon.

Essentially, Paul repeated in the Onesimus example an earlier message that he wrote to the Galatians: individuals who believe in Christ are all children of God. There is neither Jew nor Greek, slave nor free, male nor female.

The Bible doesn't mention the outcome of Paul's request of Philemon. Apparently, Philemon was lenient with Onesimus. Likely, he gave Onesimus his freedom. Ecclesiastical tradition represented Onesimus as the first bishop of the Berean church. He was martyred, along with Philemon, during the general persecution of the Christian church under Emperor Nero.

Reflection

Given Onesimus's treatment of his master, Philemon, was Paul's request to Philemon for leniency just or unjust? Explain your answer.

Bilhah and Zilpah, Slaves, Servants, or Wives? (Genesis 29:16–35, 30:1–24, 33:1–7, 35:23–26)

Heart of the Story

The twelve tribes of Jacob would have been the eight tribes without Bilhah and Zilpah. Although Jacob sired two boys with each servant, he didn't value them as highly as he valued his wives.

Story Line

Leah and Rachel were Laban's daughters; both married Jacob. Jacob loved Rachel and resented Leah. He married Leah only because Laban tricked him. Following Middle Eastern marriage custom, Laban gave both daughters a maidservant when they married. Leah's maid was named Zilpah, and Rachel's was Bilhah. Some Bible scholars believe that Zilpah was younger than Bilhah. Laban gave the younger Zilpah to Leah to further Jacob's wedding night belief that he married Rachel, the younger sister.

When Rachel realized she was barren, she gave Bilhah to Jacob to have children in her name. In doing so, she followed the example of Sarah giving her servant Hagar to Abraham to bear a son in Sarah's name. Outcomes of Jacob and Bilhah's unions were two sons, Dan and Naphtali. After having four sons, Leah stopped conceiving. Then, Leah gave Zilpah to Jacob to bear children in her name. Subsequently, Zilpah bore Jacob two sons, Gad and Asher.

In Old Testament times, it was acceptable for a maidservant to conceive children with a barren wife's husband. Some ancient cultures, i.e., Nuzi, provided written instructions that a wife had full authority over the children. Rachel and Leah named their maidservant's sons.

Both Bilhah and Zilpah had their own tent in Jacob's camp. They were Jacob's concubines or secondary wives. Despite Bilhah and Zilpah's sons being adopted by Rachel and Leah, they were associated with their birth mothers. In the official biblical record of Jacob's children (Genesis 35:25–26), Bilhah was listed as the mother of Dan and Naphtali. Zilpah was named the mother of Gad and Asher. The sons of Bilhah and Zilpah lived in their mother's tent, similar to Leah's and Rachel's children living with their mothers.

Jacob didn't value Bilhah, Zilpah, and their sons as highly as he valued Leah, Rachel, and their sons. When he saw Esau coming with four hundred men, Jacob was afraid that Esau would kill him and his family. Jacob spread out the family, with Bilhah and Zilpah and their sons positioned first. Leah and her sons were positioned second. Rachel and Joseph were in the rear and farthest from potential harm from Esau. If Bilhah's and Zilpah's sons were truly the son of Leah and Rachel, Jacob would have integrated them with their adoptive mothers rather than place them first in the family column.

Pondering Relationships

Bilhah and Zilpah had little voice in what happened to them in either Laban's household or in Jacob's. For example, Laban *gave* Zilpah to Leah when she married Jacob and gave Bilhah to Rachel when she married Jacob. Similarly, Rachel *gave* Bilhap to Jacob as a concubine and Leah gave Zilpah to Jacob as a concubine.

In none of these instances does the Bible give even a hint that either maidservant had a voice about who they served or accepted to father their children. Some early Bible translations used the word *slave girl* rather than maidservant to describe the positions of Bilhah and Zilpah in Laban's and Jacob's households. Considering that both Laban and Jacob's wives gave these maidservants to another person, slave is the better descriptor of Bilhah's and Zilpah's position in both households.

Leah's and Rachel's giving their maidservants to Jacob to bear children in their name seems abhorrent. As women, we ask how Leah and Rachel could have been so self-absorbed. Yet, Laban's family had a pattern of viewing servants as a commodity. Apparently, Jacob accepted this same view of women servants. He made no objection to having sex with Bilhah or Zilpah. Jacob was the spiritual head of his household. Supposedly, Jacob led his wives, sons, and servants in ways of godly behavior; nevertheless, we see Jacob's actions at best reflecting cultures around him, and at worst not standing for God's justice.

For several reasons, Bilhah and/or Zilpah could have willingly become Jacob's concubine and mother of his sons. First, each may have loved their mistress and wanted to help and please her. Second, both could have been attracted to the man, Jacob. Third, the maids could have reasoned that a child fathered by Jacob would have a birthright status not open to a child sired by another servant/slave. Finally, as the mother of Jacob's sons, they would have greater status and security within Jacob's household.

After Bilhah and Zilpah birthed sons to Jacob, Leah and Rachel conceived children. Leah bore two additional sons and a daughter. Rachel gave birth to Joseph and Benjamin. Rachel's intense longing for and happiness when she birthed her own sons suggested she was partial to Joseph and Benjamin over Dan and Naphtali.

Both Bilhah and Zilpah knew the family history of Sarah, insisting that Hagar and Ishmael be expelled from Abraham's camp after Isaac was born. In particular, Bilhah would have taken care not to offend Jacob's favorite wife, Rachel. She wanted Dan and Naphtali to retain their position as sons in Jacob's household.

Reflection

The Bible recorded when Leah and Rachel died and where they were buried. There is no such record of the deaths and burial of Zilpah and Bilhah. What does this absence say about the status of Zilpah and Bilhap?

Gehazi, Greedy Servant
(2 Kings 5:19–27)
Heart of the Story

Gehazi was Elisha's personal servant for many years. Deliberately, he disobeyed Elisha for his own gain.

Story Line

Gehazi lived with Elisha on Mount Carmel and went with him on Elisha's tours throughout Israel. He was with Elisha when the Aram war commander, Naaman, came to Elisha to be cured of leprosy. Probably, Gehazi conveyed Elisha's message to Naaman that he needed to wash seven times in the Jordan River. After he was cured, Naaman returned to Elisha and offered him gifts and money. Gehazi listened when Elisha assured Naaman that he wanted no payment or reward for Naaman's cure.

Unfortunately, greedy Gehazi ran after Naaman. In Elisha's name, Gehazi asked for payment for curing Naaman. Gehazi specified items that were part of Naaman's caravan, i.e., a talent of silver and two sets of clothes. Gladly, Naaman gave the money and clothes to Gehazi. Gehazi returned to Elisha's house where he hid the gifts.

When Gehazi went into the prophet, Elisha asked him where he had been. Gehazi denied that he went anywhere; however, Elisha knew otherwise. Elisha's spirit was with Gehazi when he went to Naaman. Elisha attempted to persuade Gehazi that curing a person of an illness wasn't the time to take money, clothes, or other gift. Apparently, Gehazi didn't agree because Elisha's next words to Gehazi were disastrous: Elisha told Gehazi that Naaman's leprosy would cling to him and his descendants forever. Immediately, Gehazi turned white with leprosy. He left Elisha's presence and employment.

Pondering Relationships

Gehazi lied to Naaman when he asked for gifts and to Elisha when he denied receiving payment from Naaman. Probably, Gehazi wasn't inherently avaricious. In the story of the Shunammite woman, Gehazi pointed out the woman's desire for a son, a nonmaterial gift. Two talents of silver and two changes of clothes were an insignificant sum when compared to a lifetime of leprosy. The value of the gifts and money didn't reflect how much Naaman came prepared to pay for his restored health.

Possibly, Gehazi acted as he did because he was biased against Arameans. Remember, he identified Naaman as "this Aramean." For years, Aram and Israel engaged in raids into each other's lands and clashed militarily. Gehazi knew Arameans took captives from Israel. He knew Naaman was their feared and successful war commander. Perhaps, a member of Gehazi family was hurt or taken captive in one of these raids.

Gehazi recognized that Elisha was the greatest prophet in Israel and proud that he was Elisha's servant. Therein could be the reason Gehazi extorted payment from Naaman. Perhaps Gehazi believed that Elisha himself performed miracles, not realizing that Elisha was only the instrument through which God acted. From this perspective, if Elisha expended energy to heal Naaman, Elisha had a right to be paid.

Reflection

Nowhere in the Bible's descriptions of the relationship between Gehazi and Elisha do we see a tender, familial relationship despite the years they spent together. What are some possible reasons for this distance?

Contemplation

Often, newer Bible translations use the word *servant*, omitting almost altogether the word *slave* in the Bible. Which do you think is the more accurate word in these six stories set in the culture/society of the ancient world? Perhaps, even in Holy Scriptures, we try to sanitize relationships and behavior. But, as Americans say, "It is what it is."

Christ told his followers that they shouldn't be like many kings and great men who were waited on by a bevy of servants; rather, the greatest among them should be like a servant (Luke 22:25–26). Christ modeled this behavior by washing his disciples' feet, an action usually completed by a slave or servant.

Most western Christians think of slavery as past, but human slavery exists in the twenty-first century. Over 35.8 million people live as slaves (Global Slavery Index, 2014). Many are in sub-Saharan Africa, the Middle East, or Asia. Most slaves today are forced laborers, prostitutes, child brides, or soldiers. Slavery is present in the United States, e.g., trafficking women and children. Because many slaves don't know Christ, they live without hope.

Pondering Relationships of Masters and Slaves/Servants

1. Why would newer translations of the Bible use the word *servant* in place of *slave*? How do you reconcile past Christians being slave owners?

2. What responsibility do Christians have to eliminate slavery in the world?

3. Sometimes we have a bad day and are tempted to take out frustrations by snapping at our spouse or children. We don't because we love them. If you had a bad day and had slaves/servants, how could they bear the brunt of your stressful day?

CHAPTER 6

Friends

Friends are connected by affection and esteem. God offers his friendship to the godly and takes them into his confidence. Abraham was God's friend, a favored companion. Moses and God were friends; they met frequently and talked. When he lived on earth, Jesus had friends. At the Last Supper, Christ told the disciples that because he shared with them everything he learned from God, they were no longer servants, but friends.

Although God should be our best friend and the first one we turn to in times of trouble, the Bible recommends that we have earthly friends. True friends strengthen us: "Two people are better off than one, for they can help each other succeed. If one person falls, the other can reach out and help. But someone who falls alone is in real trouble" (Ecclesiastes 4:9–10 NLT). "A person standing alone can be attacked and defeated, but two can stand back-to-back and conquer. Three are even better for a triple-braided cord is not easily broken" (Ecclesiastes 4:12 NLT).

The book of Proverbs provides criteria for friends. Friends remain loyal in the best of times and the worst of times; when we are praised and when we are maligned; when we succeed and when we fail. Friends are dependable and steadfast. They are individuals who may be in our life from grade school into old age. Wounds from a sincere friend are better than many kisses (praise) from an enemy. Friends share truths about us and our situations that may be uncomfortable to hear; but, when offered by a friend, they are never meant to harm or demean. Friends give good advice, not advice that leads us astray or into wrong thinking and doing. Simply put, friends love us for being us. They care about our character more than they care about our worldly success.

Present-day Christians need to think before they accept a person as a friend. Some "friends" can destroy us outright or have a negative influence on our Christian walk and witness. God said not to befriend angry persons or to associate with hot-tempered people. Why? If we do, we will become like them and endanger our soul. Likewise, Christians should avoid troublemakers who plant seeds of conflict and avoid gossips who can separate friends.

Christ summarized friendship when he said that there is no greater love than a man who gives his life for his friend. While we were still God's enemies, our friendship with God was restored by the death of his son. As you read stories in this chapter, ponder how the six men demonstrated friendship. I arranged the stories from the best-acting friend to the worst-acting one. What made them good or not-so-good friends? Compare and contrast their actions against God's criteria for friendship. What can you learn about friendship behavior from these Bible examples?

- Hushai, King David's friend
- Ebed-Melech, Jeremiah's friend
- Tychicus, Paul's friend and companion
- Job's friends
- Hirah, friend of Judah
- Jonadab, prince Amnon's shrewd friend

Hushai, King David's Friend (1 Chronicles 27:33; 2 Samuel 15:13–37, 16:15–17)

Heart of the Story

Hushai was King David's friend. He was also a double agent—he was loyal to King David, but entered Absalom's court as a counselor.

Story Line

When Chronicles listed King David's royal court, Ahithophel was identified as the king's counselor. Hushai was simply identified as David's friend. Some commentators asserted that "friend" was a formal court title, i.e., secretary of state. While others argued that "friend" was a simple noun. Hushai was David's confidante and intimate companion. Hushai's name means "quick" or "a gift of brotherhood." This Benjaminite was both quick and closer than any brother to King David.

When David's son, Prince Absalom declared himself king, David fled Jerusalem with his household and close fighting men. David walked barefoot up the Mount of Olives, weeping. His head was covered in grief. As he climbed, David received updates from loyal men. One update included that his chief counselor, Ahithophel, was a coconspirator with Absalom. Immediately, David prayed that God would turn Ahithophel's counsel into foolishness.

At the top of the Mount of Olives, Hushai met David. Hushai's robe was torn, and he had dust on his head to demonstrate oneness with David's grief. Although an elderly man, Hushai was determined to go into exile with King David. Ever the strategist, David had another plan for his friend. David asked Hushai to return to Jerusalem, join Absalom's court, and thwart Ahithophel's advice. While in the royal palace, Hushai could hear Absalom's plans and relay them to David through couriers.

Pondering Relationships

When Hushai walked into Absalom's court and cried, "Long live the king," Absalom challenged him, saying, "Is this the love you show your friend? Why didn't you go with your friend?" (2 Samuel 16:16–17 NIV). Hushai assured Absalom that his loyalty and service was to the king of Israel, not to a man. Apparently, Absalom believed Hushai.

Shortly afterward, Absalom asked Ahithophel and Israel's elders what should be done about David. Ahithophel volunteered to lead an elite cadre of twelve thousand men to attack David immediately, while David was weary and weak. Then, Ahithophel would return the remainder of the royal household to Jerusalem.

Absalom wasn't satisfied with Ahithophel's strategy. Perhaps, Absalom feared that if Ahithophel killed David, Ahithophel would usurp his power base, which was still shaky. King Absalom summoned Hushai and asked his advice.

After hearing Ahithophel's plan, Hushai said that it would fail for two reasons: First, Ahithophel wouldn't find David. David was canny enough not to spend nights with his men. Second, David's fighters were seasoned. Absalom's twelve thousand soldiers would be slaughtered by David's men. Hushai pointed out that if Israelite soldiers heard that Absalom's troops were decimated, they would fear David and his brave fighters.

Hushai proposed an alternative plan: that King Absalom recruit men from all Israelite tribes and lead the soldiers into battle against David. Absalom and Israel's elders preferred Hushai's plan. It maintained King Absalom's position as leader of the army and allowed each of the twelve tribes of Israel to have a part in the campaign against David.

Two important events occurred immediately after Absalom accepted Hushai's advice. First, Hushai sent word to David about Absalom's plan. He advised David to cross to the east side of the Jordan River where he would be safer. Second, Ahithophel went home, put his house in order, and hung himself. Ahithophel realized that Hushai's plan gave David time to consolidate his fighting force. He knew David would regain the throne of Israel and kill him for his part in Absalom's conspiracy.

Reflection

The role Hushai played to protect and restore David to Israel's throne can't be overestimated. How would you describe and evaluate Hushai's friendship to King David?

Ebed-Melech, Jeremiah's Friend
(Jeremiah 38:1–13, 39:15–18)

Heart of the Story

An Ethiopian eunuch in King Zedekiah's household, Ebed-Melech was one of a handful of Jeremiah's friends in the final days before the fall of Jerusalem.

Story Line

The first time the Bible identified Ebed-Melech, Jeremiah was in a cistern in the guard's courtyard. Jeremiah was put there by King Zedekiah's order after powerful courtiers accused him of treason. Jeremiah's "treason" consisted of relaying God's words that Jerusalem would be given into the hands of the Babylonians. Inhabitants who remained in the city would die by sword, famine, and pestilence. In contrast, inhabitants who left Jerusalem and surrendered to the Babylonians would live.

A cistern is a collection chamber that gathers surface water. In ancient Jerusalem, most cisterns were dug in the ground. They were bell-shaped like a 1960s-era glass milk bottle, the top narrowed so water wouldn't evaporate. Very little light filtered through the narrow opening at the cistern top. In wealthy homes, cistern sides were sometimes coated with plaster; however, often they were plain mud. In the guard courtyard, the cistern was empty of water. Jeremiah sat and slept in the mud that accumulated at the bottom of the cistern.

Ebed-Melech went to the Benjamin Gate where King Zedekiah held court. In front of the court, Ebed-Melech told the king that Jeremiah's accusers were evil men. They put Jeremiah in a cistern pit where he would die of starvation. Ebed-Melech asked Zedekiah if he could take Jeremiah from the cistern. Zedekiah agreed and gave Ebed-Melech thirty men to assist him and ensure that no one blocked Jeremiah's rescue.

After Ebed-Melech pulled Jeremiah from the muddy cistern, Jeremiah remained in the courtyard of the guard until Jerusalem fell to the Babylonians. He was given bread to eat as long as the Jerusalem bread supply lasted. During this time, Jeremiah was allowed visitors. God gave Jeremiah a message for Ebed-Melech: although the disaster that Ebed-Melech feared would fall on Jerusalem, Ebed-Melech need not fear. Because Ebed-Melech trusted God, he wouldn't be killed nor given into the hands of the Babylonians.

Pondering Relationships

Ebed-Melech means "servant of the king." Possibly, he was a slave. Like many Bible eunuchs, he had substantial duties in the royal court. It took great courage for Ebed-Melech to go where King Zedekiah held public court and accuse Jeremiah's persecutors of acting wickedly. Ebed-Melech was a servant/slave while the four men who put Jeremiah in the cistern were senior officials, possibly even princes, in the king's court.

Before Ebed-Melech removed Jeremiah from the cistern, he obtained old rags and worn-out clothes. He lowered the rags and clothes into the cistern and told Jeremiah to wrap them around his arms and to pad the ropes used to lift Jeremiah. Not only was Ebed-Melech concerned about getting Jeremiah out of the cistern, Ebed-Melech was careful not to hurt Jeremiah as he pulled Jeremiah upward. The Bible doesn't identify how long Jeremiah was in the dark, muddy cistern, nor if he was fed during this confinement. Lack of food, water, and sunshine could have caused Jeremiah to be emaciated and his bones brittle.

Ebed-Meleh believed Jeremiah's prophecy that Jerusalem would fall to the Babylonians and many of its people would be murdered. As a palace servant, he expected to be killed outright or taken captive to Babylon. In a similar position, many individuals would be concerned only with living comfortably while they could. Few servants would have jeopardized their standing with the king, or made enemies of senior officials, by championing Jeremiah. Most of the royal court despised Jerimiah and his message.

Reflection

"A friend is always loyal" (Proverbs 17:17 NLT). Is there anyone you are *always* loyal to? Take the time to name these specific friends in your life.

Tychicus, Paul's Friend and Companion
(Acts 20:4–6; Ephesians 6:21–2;
Colossians 4:7–9; 2 Timothy 4:12; Titus 3:12)

Heart of the Story

Tychicus had the spiritual gift of encouragement, which he used to build up early Christian churches. Tychicus was Paul's voice to the churches at Ephesus and Colossae.

Story Line

Snippets of information about Tychicus are found in five New Testament books: Acts, Ephesians, Colossians, 2 Timothy, and Titus. He was Paul's close friend, valued helper, and loyal to the end of Paul's life. Tychicus was from Asia Minor. Likely, Tychicus met Paul on Paul's second missionary journey, when Paul spent a short time in Ephesus. Their relationship deepened when Paul stayed in Ephesus during his third missionary journey. Tychicus represented the Asian churches when Paul took a monetary collection to Jerusalem from the largely Gentile churches in Asia and Greece.

Tychicus was with Paul when Paul was on house arrest in Rome. During the two-year confinement, Paul wrote letters (around AD 60) to the Ephesian, Philippian, and Colossian churches and the personal letter to Philemon. Tychicus delivered the letters to the churches at Ephesus and Colossae. In his letters, Paul named Tychicus a dear brother, fellow minister, and faithful servant. He assured the Ephesians and Colossians that Tychicus would tell them about his welfare. Tychicus had intimate knowledge of Paul's circumstances in Rome and would share it with church members when and where appropriate.

Pondering Relationships

In his letters to the Colossian and Ephesian churches, Paul stated that Tychicus would encourage their hearts. The Amplified Bible translated *encourage* as "console and cheer and encourage and strengthen" (Ephesians 6:22). Members of the Ephesus and Colossae churches were young in the faith. They needed both guidance and encouragement.

In particular, the Colossian church was attacked by heretics. They introduced several add-ons, i.e., asceticism, angel worship, and secret knowledge, to the gospel of salvation by grace. The situation was so dire that Colossian church founder, Epaphras, traveled to Rome to consult Paul. The result was Paul's letter to the Colossian church. Paul sent the doctrinally clear Tychicus to strengthen believers at Colossae.

When Paul wrote to the church at Rome, he identified that Christians were one body in Christ, and went on to say that different members had different gifts according to God's grace. One of the gifts that Paul mentioned was encouragement. When Paul called Tychicus an "encourager," he meant that Tychicus possessed the spiritual gift of encouragement. Tychicus could both teach and exhort church members to greater accomplishments in their walk with Christ.

As Christians, we should look for friends among individuals who share our worldview; but, that isn't always easy. Many times we have jobs where there are few, if any, Christians. My first job was in a strange city. My workplace friends were non-Christians. Although we talked about work, boyfriends, our profession, etc., we never talked about God or Christian beliefs. My conversations and thoughts became like theirs. Perhaps, like Tychicus, I consoled and cheered them; however, I didn't encourage their Christian faith. Paul wouldn't have sent me to young churches or young Christians who needed guidance and strengthening in the faith.

In addition to his other virtues, e.g., encouragement, loyalty, faithfulness, Tychicus submitted to Paul's headship and authority in the Christian church. Tychicus went where Paul thought his leadership was most needed. Paul wrote to Titus that he would send either Tychicus or Artemus to oversee the church on Crete, so Titus could join him in Rome (Titus 3:12). Apparently, Tychicus was with Paul at the beginning of his second (and last) imprisonment in Rome (AD 66–67). Later, Paul sent Tychicus to Ephesus to minister there.

Reflection

"A friend loves at all times" (Proverbs 17:17 NIV). Is love a rational requirement for friendship? Have you ever had a friend you really didn't like, let alone love?

Job's Friends
(Job 1–5)

Heart of the Story

Rather than comfort Job following his devastating losses, Job's friends told Job that he brought them on himself by sinning.

Story Line

The book of Job tells the story of a non-Israelite man who lived in Uz, an area now located in Jordan. He was the greatest and richest man in the East. Job lived in the second millennium (2000–1000 BC) before Christ's birth. Some scholars believed Job was a contemporary of Abraham. Job worshiped and feared Yahweh. He was blameless, upright, and shunned evil.

Satan hated Job and asked God's permission to test him. Confident that Job would maintain his integrity, God allowed Satan to do anything to Job except kill him. The result was that Satan killed Job's children, ruined his crops, robbed him of all livestock, destroyed his home, and afflicted Job's body with severe sores and boils. Job was reduced to abject poverty.

Job's three friends—Eliphaz, Bildad, and Zophar—heard of Job's losses and came to comfort him. When the friends saw Job sitting on an ash heap, they hardly recognized him. Boils and skin lesions covered every inch of Job's body. The men wept aloud, tore their robes, and sprinkled ashes on their head to demonstrate their shared grief. For seven days, the three friends sat on the ground with Job. None said a word because they saw how great Job suffered.

The seven days the friends sat with Job and their silence were important. Seven days is the traditional amount of time close friends and family grieve for an individual who died. Perhaps, Job's friends were acknowledging the death of his ten children. On the other hand, they grieved the death of Job's way of life, including his health. The three friend's silence could be interpreted in three ways. First, it could mean they were too stunned to speak when they saw Job's devastated life. Second, the silence implied that they knew words weren't much help in this situation. Third, their silence may have been the courtesy of the Near East, where the host speaks first to guests.

Job's discourse that he cursed the day he was born started three rounds of speeches between Job and his friends. The first to speak was Eliphaz, followed by Bildad, then Zophar. Because Eliphaz spoke first, he was probably the oldest and wisest of the three friends. Eliphaz offered the profoundest, gentlest, and kindest comments to Job; however, all three friends contended that Job sinned to warrant such divine punishment. Job's friends agreed that the simultaneous nature of Job's losses couldn't have occurred through natural means.

Pondering Relationships

Job's friends used the Near Eastern doctrine of reward and punishment to explain Job's losses. Today, some Christians still believe that unfavorable life events are God's punishment for sin. It is easier to blame God rather than accept that we reap the consequences of our bad decisions, e.g., we drove twenty miles over the speed limit and had to pay a 150 dollar speeding ticket.

Job's story illustrates that what occurs in the physical world may reflect far greater conflicts in the spiritual world. Satan attacked Job because he was a righteous, God-fearing man. Job is an early Old Testament model for Christians today. He demonstrated how Christians can seek and talk to God when trials come their way. In his confusion and agony, Job turned to God rather than his friends for advice.

The epilogue of Job described God rebuking the three friends because they didn't correctly represent him to Job. The Bible didn't identify how the friends erred. Perhaps, their offense was speaking about God rather than to God. Perhaps, the three friends didn't have true knowledge of the living God, whose behavior they attempted to explain. God required that the friends offer sacrifices for their own sins, and that Job pray that God would forgive them.

Reflection

"Many will say they are loyal friends, but who can find one who is truly reliable?" (Proverbs 20:6 NLT). How were Job's friends reliable or not reliable? What about you, are you a reliable friend?

Hirah, Friend of Judah
(Genesis 38)

Heart of the Story

Judah's friend, Hirah, played a role in Judah marrying a Canaanite woman and Judah getting his daughter-in-law pregnant.

Story Line

Fleeing Jacob's inconsolable grief over the supposed death of Joseph, Judah left Hebron, traveled south, and stayed with his friend, Hirah. Hirah was a Canaanite who lived in Adullam. The size of Adullam in 1900 BC isn't known; however, 450 years later when Joshua conquered Canaan, Adullam had its own king. Hirah meant "splendor," which suggests that Hirah was part of the ruling class of Adullam. Possibly, Judah was flattered to be Hirah's friend and to stay in his home.

While living with Hirah, Judah married a Canaanite woman. Judah's wife was not named. She was simply called the daughter of Shua. Judah's wife bore him three sons, Er, Onan, and Shelah. Shelah was born at Keri, located an even further distance from Jacob's home at Hebron. Possibly, Judah didn't return to, or live with Jacob, during these married years.

When Er grew to adulthood, Judah obtained a Canaanite wife for him. Her name was Tamar. Er died. Following ancient marriage customs, Tamar became the wife of Onan. Onan was to secure the deceased Er's inheritance by having a son with Tamar. But, Onan also died. The Bible recorded that both Er and Onan died because they were wicked; however, Judah feared that Tamar was some type of "black widow."

Judah sent Tamar back to her father's home, saying that when Shelah grew up, Tamar could become his wife. When Shelah became an adult, Judah didn't contact Tamar to marry him. Tamar's childless state left her helpless and socially disadvantaged. In the ancient Near East, a son cared for his mother after the father's death. Generally, a widowed mother lived with the eldest son.

Eventually, Judah's wife died and Judah grieved her passing. When he recovered, Judah went to Timnah where his sheep were being sheared. Hirah, who remained Judah's friend through all of these years, went with Judah. On the outskirts of Enaim, Judah and Hirah came upon a veiled woman. Believing she was a shrine prostitute, Judah propositioned her. He agreed to give her a young goat for her services. Because Judah had no goat with him, he left his seal, cord, and staff with the woman, saying that the next day he would send her a goat for payment and reclaim the items.

The next day when Hirah took the goat to Enaim, he couldn't find the prostitute. When Hirah inquired of the townsmen, he learned that Enaim never had a shrine prostitute. Hirah went back to Judah and told him the full story. Afraid that he would become a laughing stock if he continued the search, Judah decided to allow the prostitute to retain his seal, cord, and staff.

From that time forward, the Bible provided no information about Hirah; however, we read that the shrine prostitute was Tamar. Tamar became pregnant from her encounter with Judah. She had twins, Perez and Zerah. Judah, Tamar, and their son Perez were ancestors of Christ.

Pondering Relationships

Hirah remained Judah's friend for twenty to thirty years. At first read, we think that a friendship that lasted that long is admirable; however, the friendship wasn't beneficial to Judah. Judah was the son of Jacob, who worshipped the true God. In contrast, Hirah worshipped a false Caananite god.

Hirah didn't act outside his society's norms; however, through his influence, Judah's behavior devolved. First, he was a friend with a pagan, then, he married one. Finally, Judah engaged in pagan immorality with what he thought was a shrine prostitute. Judah became more concerned with being laughed at than retrieving symbols of his individual and clan identity. Reading the story makes me wonder if Hirah wasn't secretly gloating at Judah's falling away from his father's faith and standards.

The brother of Christ, James, asked the question, "Don't you realize that friendship with the world makes you an enemy of God?" (James 4:4 NLT). He went on to say that anyone who chooses to be a friend of the world becomes an enemy of God. Notice James's use of the word "choose." We have the option—it is up to us—to choose, or not choose, to be world-friendly. Judah chose the world when he went to live with his friend, Hirah.

God promised Abraham that the world's redeemer (Messiah) would come through his descendants. Christ came through Judah's offspring. As Satan's instrument, Hirah encouraged Judah to turn from the true God and tried to sever Judah's central place in the Messiah's ancestry. Judah's friendship with Hirah is a reminder not to cut ouselves off from church family, as Judah cut himself off from his father and brothers.

Reflection

Are any of your friends enemies of God, even if that enmity is expressed as indifference?

Jonadab, Prince Amnon's Shrewd Friend
(2 Samuel 13)

Heart of the Story

Prince Amnon's friend, Jonadab, gave him advice that led to King David's sons being killed and David being dethroned temporarily.

Story Line

Jonadab was King David's nephew and a friend of Prince Amnon, King David's heir. One day Jonadab asked Amnon why he looked so haggard morning after morning. Amnon admitted that he was in love with Tamar but couldn't possess her. Tamar was David's daughter and Amnon's half sister. Mosaic law said a man couldn't have sex with the daughter of his father's wife.

The Bible called Jonadab a "shrewd" man. The Hebrew word was *châkâm*, which translates as subtle and cunning (Strong, 2010). In English, the archaic meaning of shrewd is mischievous, harmful, and dangerous. Certainly, what Jonadab proposed next was both cunning and harmful. Jonadab advised Amnon to pretend to be sick. When King David visited him, Amnon should request that Tamar come to his home and prepare, and serve him bread; thus, Amnon would get his beautiful sister alone.

The plan proceeded exactly as Jonadab counseled. David indulged his heir and sent Tamar to wait on him. When Tamar tried to flee Amnon's unwanted attentions, he brutally raped her. His lust satisfied, Amnon expelled Tamar from his home. Devastated and weeping, Tamar went to Absalom's (her full brother) home. Absalom advised Tamar to keep silent about the rape; however, King David and the entire court knew Amnon raped Tamar. Certainly, Jonadab knew his plan succeeded.

For two years, Absalom neither said nor did anything toward Amnon for raping Tamar. It's tempting to speculate whether or not Jonadab's role in the planned rape was public knowledge. Indulged, demanding Amnon doesn't seem the type to keep Jonadab's role a secret, if telling it absolved him from some responsibility for the heinous act. Can't you hear Prince Ammon say, "It was all cousin Jonadab's idea"?

Then, Absalom invited Amnon and his other half brothers and sisters to his country home to celebrate his sheepshearing. At a banquet, Absalom had Amnon murdered. He allowed his other brothers and sisters to return home. Absalom fled to his mother's family in Geshur.

Before David's children returned to Jerusalem, David received word that Absalom killed all of them. As David began to grieve, Jonadab spoke up saying that only Amnon was dead. Jonadab alleged that it was Absalom's plan all along to kill Amnon because he raped Tamar. Soon the watchman saw many people coming toward Jerusalem. When the watchman told David that his children were alive, Jonadab didn't hesitate to say, "I told you so."

Pondering Relationships

It's tempting to wonder why Jonadab wasn't at Absalom's sheepshearing celebration. Maybe, Absalom didn't invite his cousin because he knew Jonadab's role in Tamar's rape. More likely, Jonadab was cunning enough to refuse Absalom's invitation.

One Bible commentator speculated that Absalom and Jonadab colluded to remove Amnon from succession to the throne (Hill, 1987). He proposed that Absalom and Jonadab recognized that Amnon was ruled by his lusts; therefore, Amnon would make a poor king. Consequently, Absalom and Jonadab set up Amnon to rape Tamar and give Absalom a reason to kill him. This interpretation explains how Jonadab knew that (a) Absalom didn't kill his other brothers and sisters, and that (b) Absalom held a grudge against Amnon for two years.

Counter-arguments are that Tamar lived in Absalom's house after the rape. Absalom loved his sister and wouldn't participate in her pain or shame. He named one of his daughters, Tamar, after his sister. When Absalom overthrew King David, the Bible doesn't identify Jonadab as one of Absalom's counselors or a member of his inner circle of friends.

Jonadab was an astute problem solver but not a loyal friend. He developed plans and gave advice without consideration for whom was hurt. An Israelite proverb is "As iron sharpens iron, so one man sharpens another" (Proverbs 27:17 NIV). The proverb means that friends mold the character of each other when they spend time together. Jonadab was Amnon's friend. Whether he contributed to Amnon's depraved behavior or vice versa, the bottom line is that together they hatched a shameful plot to rape Princess Tamar. They sharpened each other, but not in a good way.

Reflection

Think about your friends and what activities you engage in with them. Does it really matter if your closest friends are Christians?

Contemplation

An American saying is, "Friendship is like a bank account; you cannot withdraw on it without making deposits." This proverb likely means friendship is a give-and-take process. If you want to take from a friendship, you must give to it. Perhaps, you must even do the giving before the taking.

What kind of friend are you—a friend like Jonadab and Hirah, or a friend like Ebed-Melech and Hushai? Do you give Christ's perspective to your friends when they ask for advice; or, do you agree with what they say no matter their course of action? No doubt, the latter action may retain the friend longer; however, it may not be consistent with Proverb's criteria for friendship.

Pondering Friend Relationships

1. What kind of friends do you want? When you ask for advice from a friend, do you just want them to agree with you, or do you want a Christian perspective on your problem or challenge?

2. Have you ever had a friend who led you away from God? How did that come about? Are the two of you still friends?

3. Having Christian friends is a choice we consciously make. How can we go about having godly friends? Do you have any friends or relationships that you need to distance yourself from? If so, who are they and how can you take needed action?

CHAPTER 7

Kings and Rulers

Before the Israelites entered the Promised Land, God gave Moses requirements for a future king over Israel. If a king kept these conditions, God promised that he and his descendants would reign over Israel a long time.

Dos and Don'ts for Kings
(Deuteronomy 17:14–20)

What an Israelite King Should Do	What an Israelite King Should Not Do
Be God's choice and an Israelite.	Acquire many horses. Send Israelites to Egypt for horses.
Write a copy of the law on a scroll.	Return to Egypt.
Keep the scroll of law with him.	Marry many wives or his heart will be led astray.
Read the scroll daily so he learn to revere God.	Accumulate large amounts of gold or silver.
Follow all God's laws and decrees.	Consider himself better than his brothers.

About 1050 BC, Israelite tribal elders visited Samuel at Ramah and asked for a king. They reminded Samuel that Moses prophesized that the time would come when Israel wanted a king.

When the elders asked Samuel for a king, Samuel took their request to God. God told Samuel that by asking for an earthly king, the Israelites rejected him as their king. God directed Samuel to explain to the Israelites how a king would negatively affect their lives. God knew everything that future Israelite kings would do, i.e., plunder the land. Samuel's final dire warning to the Israelite leaders was that eventually they would become the king's slaves. When this happened, they would cry out to God; but, God wouldn't answer them (1 Samuel 8:18–20).

Despite these explanations and warnings, Israelite tribal elders persisted in asking for a king. Finally, God agreed to give them one. Chapter 7 encompasses the stories of six kings who ruled the Israelites. They are discussed in chronological order, beginning with Abimelech and ending with Herod Agrippa I. Although lesser know, most lived and ruled at a crucial time. They powerfully impacted Israelite history.

Most of these six rulers and other Israelite kings took more from than they gave to subjects. Some were merely inept. Others were openly narcissistic and cared only for their own comfort. One was crowned before God established the Israelite monarchy. For a brief time, a woman ruled Judah. See what you can learn about good and bad rulers from these six characters:

• King Abimelech, Gideon's son.

- Ish-Bosheth, shameful king.
- Athaliah, woman ruler of Judah.
- Hoshea, last king of Israel.
- Jehoiachin, captive king.
- Herod Agrippa I, proclaimed a god.

King Abimelech, Gideon's Son
(Judges 9)

Heart of the Story

Judges chapter 9 contains fifty-seven riveting verses of the rise and fall of the first Israelite king in the Promised Land.

Story Line

After Gideon defeated the Midian army, some Israelites wanted to make him king. Gideon refused. He said that neither he nor his sons would rule over the Israelites; rather, God would rule over them. Gideon, his wives, and seventy sons lived in Orphah in West Manasseh. Gideon had one son by a concubine. The concubine's son was Abimelech, which means "my father is king." Abimelech lived in Shechem with his mother's family.

When Gideon died, Abimelech and a band of adventurers killed all but Gideon's youngest son. Men of the towns of Shechem, Beth Millo, and Thebez made Abimelech their king. After several years, God sent an evil spirit between King Abimelech and the Shechemites. When a man named Gaal moved into Shechem, many men started to follow him. One day, while Gaal and his followers were eating and drinking, they cursed Abimelech.

Abimelech heard about their disrespect and attacked Gaal and Shechem. After a fierce battle, he captured Shechem and burned its tower with over one thousand men and women in it. Abimelech scattered salt on the ground around Shechem so the soil could no longer produce farm and garden plants.

Then, King Abimelech went to Thebez and captured the town. When he attacked Thebez's strong tower, a woman inside the tower dropped a millstone. The millstone cracked Abimelech's skull. Reluctant for a woman to receive credit for his death, Abimelech persuaded his servant to kill him. When Abimelech's followers saw that he was dead, they went home. Thus, ended the short three-to-five-year reign of the first king of Israel.

Pondering Relationships

King Abimelech was a disaster, not because he was the son of a concubine; but, because the foundation of his kingship was the slaughter of his brothers. Further, his followers were paid adventurers. The Shechemites gave Abimelech money to pay these men from the temple of Baal-Berith; Baal-Berith was a Canaanite idol depicted as a fly.

Perhaps after becoming king, Abimelech had time to reflect on his status. True, he was undisputed king because he killed all opposition; however, his backers were mercenaries not known for loyalty. They condoned the murder of the sons of the man (Gideon), who freed them from the rapacious Midianites. How secure was Abimelech's throne? How likely was his son to succeed him as king? These types of insecurities caused King Abimelech to overreact when some of his drunken subjects disparaged him and his rule.

Men who lived in the towns that Abimelech ruled also had second thoughts. They remembered Gideon's words that God, not a man, should rule over them. They realized they couldn't trust a ruler who slaughtered his brothers.

The Bible ended the story of the first king of Israel by saying that God repaid Abimelech for murdering his brothers. Further, God made the men of Shechem pay for their wickedness.

Reflection

W. R. Inge (1860–1954) wrote, "A man may build a throne of bayonets, but he cannot sit on it" (Esar, 1968). How does that apply to King Abimelech?

Ish-Bosheth, Shameful King
(2 Samuel 2:8–11, 3:6–11, 4)

Heart of the Story

Ish-Bosheth's reign over Israel was propped up by Abner, commander of the military. After Abner was killed, Ish-Bosheth's own men murdered him.

Story Line

The first monarch of the twelve tribes of Israel, King Saul, and three sons died in the Battle of Mount Gilboa against the Philistines. Saul's youngest son, Ish-Bosheth, either escaped the Philistine slaughter or wasn't present at the battle. Perhaps, Saul ordered Ish-Bosheth to remain at home as a safety net for his dynasty. After Saul's death, Abner, Saul's cousin and commander of the Israelite army, established Ish-Bosheth as king over Israel. By this time, Judah seceded from the rule of Saul's house and proclaimed David king.

Originally, Ish-Bosheth's name was Esh-baal. Bible chroniclers changed it to Ish-Bosheth possibly because Esh-baal sounded too much like Baal, a false deity worshipped in Old Testament times. *Ish* means "great man", while *boshet* means "given to bashfulness, humility, or sensitive to shame" (2 Samuel 2:8 NIV).

Ish-Bosheth was born around 1047 BC. Likely, he became king when he was about forty years of age. Alternatively, some scholars believe Ish-Bosheth started to rule when he was thirty-two to thirty-three years old. From this perspective, Ish-Bosheth's reign equaled that of David's reign over Judah at Hebron, i.e., seven and a half years. Probably, Ish-Bosheth never sired children. His court was at Mahanaim, east of the Jordan River and outside Philistine threat.

As the war between the houses of Saul and David continued, David became stronger. In Israel, Abner increased his influence with the northern tribes. Afraid that Abner wanted his throne, Ish-Bosheth accused Abner of having an affair with Saul's concubine, Rizpah. In Old Testament Israel, significance was attached to having sexual relations with a king's widow(s) and concubine(s) (2 Samuel 16:21; 1 Kings 2:20–25). If Ish-

Bosheth's accusation was true, then Abner conspired to seize the kingship from him. Vehemently, Abner denied Ish-Bosheth's allegation; however, Ish-Bosheth didn't take back his words or apologize for them. The result was that deeply-offended Abner worked to turn the Israelite kingdom over to David.

Soon afterward, David's commander, Joab, murdered Abner. After Abner's death, Ish-Bosheth was afraid to continue as king. All Israel was alarmed. They knew that Abner's strength, not the king's strength strength, protected them.

Pondering Relationships

Ish-Bosheth may not have known Samuel, but he knew that Samuel anointed his father as king of Israel. Very likely, Saul repeated Samuel's requirement for a king of Israel to his sons, i.e., the king should write a scroll of the law, keep the scroll with him, read it daily, and follow God's laws and decrees. Reasons Ish-Bosheth disregarded God's requirement could have been a sense of entitlement bred into him as a royal son in Saul's court, personal pride, or obsession with personal and national safety. Nowhere do we read that Ish-Bosheth sought God or turned to God for advice.

Two of Ish-Bosheth's captains, the brothers Recab and Baanah, entered Ish-Bosheth's bedroom while he rested at noon. They stabbed Ish-Bosheth in the stomach, then cut off his head. Recab and Baanah took the head to King David, expecting David to commend them. Instead, David called them wicked and averred that they killed an innocent man on his own bed! David ordered his men to kill Recab and Baanah.

David buried Ish-Bosheth's head in Abner's tomb at Hebron. The Bible provides no information on where the remainder of Ish-Bosheth's body was buried. Likely, it was somewhere around Mahanaim. Ish-Bosheth's body wasn't placed in Saul's family tomb at Zela, Benjamin, where Saul and his three sons were buried.

Reflection

The second king in Saul's dynasty, Ish-Bosheth, didn't inspire loyalty or support. How does a leader generate loyalty in followers? Is position, e.g., minister, parent, CEO, sufficient to inspire loyalty?

Athaliah, Woman Ruler of Judah
(2 Chronicles 22:10–23:15)

Heart of the Story

When King Ahaziah was murdered, his mother, Athaliah, became ruler of Judah by killing her grandchildren. She missed one. Six years later Joash (Jehoash) was declared king.

Story Line

Athaliah was the daughter of King Ahab and Queen Jezebel of Israel. Her marriage to King Jehoram of Judah formed a political alliance between the two countries. Like her parents, Athaliah worshiped the Phoenician god, Baal Melqart, a sun and nature god. She built a temple to Baal in Jerusalem and introduced his worship into Judah.

At this time in Judah's history, four factors combined to reduce the size of the house of David. First, Athaliah's husband murdered his brothers. Second, with the exception of Ahaziah, Athaliah's sons were killed by marauding Arabs. Third, the king of Israel killed King Ahaziah and forty-two members of Judah's royal family. Fourth, when Athaliah learned that her son, King Ahaziah was dead, she killed his children, her own grandchildren. Then, she declared herself ruler of Judah.

One of Ahaziah's sons, Joash, was saved from Athaliah's deadly rampage. His aunt, Jehosheba, stole him from the royal nursery, before he could be murdered. Jehosheba was married to Jehoiada, high priest in Solomon's temple. Jehoiada hid Joash and his nurse in a temple bedroom. When Jehosheba took Joash from the royal nursery, he was about one year old and not weaned.

The next six years, Jehoiada waited, while Athaliah ruled Judah. When Joash was seven years old, Jehoiada staged a coup against Athaliah. From every town in Judah, he assembled Levites and heads of Israelite families. He made a covenant with military commanders to support Joash. On a Sabbath day, they assembled at Solomon's temple. Because Athaliah was a Baal worshiper, she paid little attention to men going into God's temple.

Jehoiada brought Joash from inside the temple, set the crown of David on his head, and presented him with a copy of the covenant that proclaimed him king. The assembled people shouted, "Long live the King." Military commanders acknowledged Joash by standing on both sides of him. Levite choirs played musical instruments, sang, and led the people in psalms. Trumpets sounded. What a wonderful celebration. A lost son of the house of David was found and declared king!

Hearing the noise, Athaliah came to Solomon's temple. She saw the crowned boy standing by a temple pillar with officers and trumpeters around him. Athaliah knew what happened. One of her grandsons lived. He was crowned the new king of Judah. She tore her robes in passion and shouted, "Treason, treason."

Pondering Relationships

Judah didn't reject Athaliah because she was a woman; but, because she was a usurper of David's throne and because of her murderous behavior. Athaliah's conduct was uncharacteristic of even the most deviant individual in history. Thinking back over my years as an adult, I remember no news stories or incidents where a grandmother intentionally killed a grandchild or multiple grandchildren. From time to time, parents kill children; but, normally grandmother's nurture, even dote on, grandchildren. Friends who are grandmothers told me that Athaliah's actions showed she was either mentally ill or possessed by Satan.

Jehoiada ordered commanders to take Athaliah outside the temple and kill her. Anyone that followed Athaliah outside was to be killed with her. When Athaliah reached the Horse Gate on the palace grounds, commanders killed her. There is no biblical record that anyone was killed with Athaliah. Not one of Athaliah's attendants or royal bodyguards was willing to die with her.

When Athaliah killed her grandchildren, she believed that the entire royal house of David was destroyed. The Davidic dynasty was ended. Now Israel could claim Judah; Judah's queen was the daughter of the former king of Israel. Despite Athaliah's evil nature, she was a pawn. Satan attempted to use Athaliah to destroy the house of David through which the Messiah was to be born.

Reflection

"The scepter of the wicked will not remain over the land allotted to the righteous, for then the righteous might use their hands to do evil" (Psalm 125:3 NIV). If the people of a nation are ruled by the wicked, will the people become wicked?

Hoshea, Last King of Israel
(2 Kings 15:29–31, 17:1–6, 18:9–10)

Heart of Story

Hoshea was the last king of the Northern Kingdom (ten tribes) of Israel. By rebelling against the king of Assyria, he caused the final destruction of Israel.

Story Line

Between 738–732 BC, Tiglath-Pileser III of Assyria conquered and annexed large areas of Israel, i.e., Galilee and Transjordan. He deported thousands of Israelites to the farthest areas of Assyria. Hoshea became king by murdering Pekah, king of Israel (732 BC). Hoshea represented a political faction that favored cooperation with Assyria, while Pekah resisted Assyria's domination. In an Assyrian record, Tiglath-Pileser III credited himself with establishing Hoshea as a vassal king in Israel. He bragged about taking ten talents of gold and one thousand talents of silver from Hoshea.

By the time Hoshea became king, Israel was a tiny nation composed of the area around Samaria. Hoshea reigned nine years (732–722 BC). In the sixth to seventh year of his reign, Tiglath-Pileser III died (726 BC). Assyria was in transition as his son, Shalmanesar V, ascended to the throne. Hoshea thought this was the ideal time to throw off Assyria's yoke. He stopped paying tribute to Assyria and contacted Egypt for aid against Assyria.

Hoshea couldn't have been more wrong. Shalmanesar V placed Hoshea in prison. Then, Shalmanesar V invaded Israel and laid siege to its capital, Samaria. In 722–721 BC, Samaria fell to Assyria. Israel's remaining citizens were deported throughout the Assyrian empire. Nothing more was heard about Hoshea. Possibly, he died of natural causes in prison. More likely, Hoshea was murdered by the vindictive Assyrians.

Pondering Relationships

The best the Bible recorded about King Hoshea is that "He did evil in the eyes of the Lord, but not like the kings of Israel that preceded him" (2 Kings 17:2 NIV). This verse warns that God's punishment comes in his time—a time that may not be at the height of an individual's or nation's ungodly behavior. Several of Israel's earlier kings were more depraved and more idolatrous than Hoshea. They sacrificed their children to worthless idols. They paid tribute to distant kings, rather than turn to God for safety and security. Despite earlier king's idolatrous behavior, God's final judgment on Israel came when Hoshea—a ruler who was less evil than many predecessors—was king.

Perhaps, part of Hoshea's sin was contacting Egypt's pharaoh for aid against Assyria. Although Hoshea didn't go to Egypt or take his people there, he turned toward Egypt and relied on Egypt. God was very explicit: the Israelites shouldn't return to Egypt. Returning to Egypt encompassed turning to Egypt for aid against national enemies.

I'm not sure what would have happened if Hoshea repented and turned to God when he became king. The Bible provides an example of King Josiah in the latter days of Judah. Josiah humbled himself. He restored Yahweh worship throughout Judah. The result was that God withheld judgment from Judah until after Josiah died. The same thing may have happened in the Northern Kingdom. God promised that if Israel repented and turned to him, he would restore them and protect them (Hosea 14).

Like most kings, Hoshea hoped to start a dynasty with sons succeeding him on Israel's throne. The Bible gives no information on Hoshea's children. Often, foreign conquerors killed children in front of their parents as a way to punish kings who opposed them. Because the Assyrians were masters of cruelty, we can hope that Hoshea had no sons for them to slaughter.

Reflection

The Bible says that Hoshea wasn't as bad as some other kings. Why didn't God destroy Israel earlier when there were worse kings?

Jehoiachin, Captive King
(2 Kings 24:8–12, 25:27–30; 2 Chronicles 36:9–10; Jeremiah 52:31–34)

Heart of the Story

Jehoiachin languished thirty-seven years in a Babylonian prison; nevertheless, he was an ancestor of Christ.

Story Line

Like so many kings of Israel and Judah, Jehoiachin had several names including Jeconiah and Coniah. His father was King Jehoiakim and his mother was Nehushta. Jehoiachin was born during the reign of his godly grandfather, King Josiah. He saw Josiah's dedication to God. The great prophet, Jeremiah, lived in Jerusalem during Jehoiachin's life. Jehoiachin knew Jeremiah's prophecy that he (Jehoiachin) would be exiled to Babylon as a consequence of his sin.

Jehoiachin became king when his father was murdered. Despite Josiah's example and Jeremiah's words, Jehoiachin did evil in God's eyes.

He acted like his father, Jehoiakim, whose kingship was rapacious, violent, and oppressive. Ezekiel described Jehoiachin as a young lion who prowled among lions and learned to catch prey and devour men (Ezekiel 19:6).

Jehoiachin was eighteen years of age when he became king of Judah; he reigned (597 BC) for three months and ten days. Then, Nebuchadnezzar and the Babylonian army came to Jerusalem. Rather than undergo a long siege, Jehoiachin surrendered. Nebuchadnezzar didn't kill Jehoiachin; instead, he deported Jehoiachin along with his mother, wives, and officials to Babylon. Nebuchadnezzar made Zedekiah, Jehoiachin's uncle, a puppet king over Judah.

When Jehoiachin arrived in Babylon, he was put in prison and remained there thirty-seven years. After Nebuchadnezzar died, his son became king. King Evil-Merodach freed Jehoiachin and honored Jehoiachin above all kings who were with him in Babylon. Jehoiachin ate at the king's table. Evil-Merodach gave Jehoiachin a regular allowance.

Pondering Relationships

The Bible provides no outward reason for Evil-Murdoch's preferential treatment to Jehoiachin. One commentator suggested that Evil-Merodach was imprisoned for a short time in his youth. In prison, he came to know Jehoiachin. Another suggested that Daniel, who was a wise man in the Babylonian court, convinced Evil-Merodach to release Jehoiachin. Perhaps, the simple explanation is that God moved the heart of Evil-Merodach to treat Jehoiachin favorably.

Evil-Merodach ruled Babylon for two years (562–560 BC). Then, he was killed by his brother-in-law, Nergal-Sharezar, who succeeded him to the throne of Babylon. Some scholars proposed that Nergal-Sharezer killed Jehoiachin because of his close association with Evil-Merodach. No evidence exists in Bible or Babylonian records that Jehoiachin died a violent death, or that he died soon after being released from prison.

After Cyrus of Persia conquered Babylon, he gave permission for the captive Jews to return to Jerusalem and rebuild God's temple. Zerubbabel was a leader who returned to Jerusalem and became governor of Judea. The Bible listed Jehoiachin as the father of Shealtiel, and Shealtiel as the father of Zerubbabel. All three are in the genealogy of Jesus Christ.

God took a really bad king, his captivity and imprisonment, and used it for good.

Reflection

Do you think that Jehoiachin repented and turned to God during his thirty-seven-year imprisonment? Remember, God said that he will redeem the wasted years for his people (Joel 2:28). Do you think that Jehoiachin's wasted years were redeemed? Can God redeem wasted relationships?

Herod Agrippa I, Proclaimed a God
(Acts 12:1–5, 20–23)

Heart of the Story

Herod Agrippa I's pride was so great that he allowed himself to be called a god—an action that caused God to kill him.

Story Line

Herod Agrippa I was born Marcus Julius Agrippa. His grandfather, Herod the Great, was responsible for the massacre of infants in Bethlehem. His father, Herod Antipas, ordered John the Baptist beheaded. Herod Agrippa I was reared in Rome, where he learned to know two youths, Caligula and Claudius. Both became emperors of Rome later in their lives. These two Roman emperors established Herod Agrippa I as king over Judea. Then, he expanded the territories he ruled. Eventually, Herod Agrippa I's kingdom encompassed Idumea through Galilee and large areas east of the Jordan River.

Flavius Josephus described Herod Agrippa I as a man who was beneficent, liberal in his gifts, and eager to oblige people (Whiston, 1987). Although perceived as being friendlier to Greeks, Herod Agrippa I observed Mosaic laws. He lived in Jerusalem much of the time and went to great lengths to appease the Jews.

King Herod Agrippa I had James, the apostle, beheaded in AD 44. Seeing that his actions pleased the Jewish leaders, Herod Agrippa I put Peter in jail. He planned to put Peter on public trial after Passover. Herod

Agrippa I assigned four soldiers to guard Peter at all times. Nonetheless, the night before Peter was scheduled for trial, God led Peter out of prison. The following morning, the soldiers had no idea where Peter was. Herod Agrippa I cross-examined the guards; he executed the soldiers when they couldn't account for Peter's absence.

Shortly afterward, Herod Agrippa I left Judea and went to Caesarea Maritima on the Mediterranean coastline. For some reason, Herod Agrippa I was angry with the people of Tyre and Sidon. City leaders met with Herod Agrippa I and asked for peace. Both Tyre and Sidon were commercial seaports. They depended on grain and other food from Judea, which Herod Agrippa I controlled.

On the second day of a festival in honor of Emperor Claudius, Herod Agrippa I wore silver clothing (Whiston, 1987). He entered the amphitheater in the morning and addressed the people. The sun reflected off his silver robes. They shone in a way that frightened his audience. After Herod Agrippa I spoke, people shouted, "This is the voice of a god, not of a man" (Acts 12:22 NIV). Herod Agrippa I made no effort to refute the people honoring him as a god, despite knowing the words were blasphemous.

The Bible recorded that immediately an angel of God struck Herod Agrippa I down because he didn't give praise to God. Josephus's narrative supplied additional information (Whiston, 1987). A severe pain developed in Herod Agrippa I's abdomen, necessitating that he be carried to his palace. Herod Agrippa I lived seven days; then he died. His insides were eaten by worms.

Pondering Relationships

The Bible seemed to conclude that Herod Agrippa I's audience identified him as a god because of his oratory skills. Josephus wrote that the audience's response was more related to Herod Agrippa I's shimmering clothes (Whiston, 1987). Probably, both were involved, as was the citizen's desire to ingratiate themselves with King Herod Agrippa I. They wanted the king to permit food supplies to be shipped to Tyre and Sidon.

We don't know how much of Herod Agrippa I's behavior was learned from his father and grandfather. At best, he knew how to play the political games necessary to stay in power in the Roman Empire. At worst, he was an egotist who, similar to his Roman emperor friends, believed it was okay to be worshiped as a god. Herod Agrippa I was a murderer. He was vindictive and withheld food from his own citizens in a fit of anger. Satan used Herod Agrippa I to obstruct the early Christian church. Nonetheless, the Acts 12 record of Herod Agrippa I ends by noting that the word of God continued to increase and spread (Acts 12:24).

Reflection

Israelites had a proverb: "When the wicked rule, the people groan" (Proverb 29:2 NIV), which applies perfectly to King Herod Agrippa I. How can bad rulers make Christians groan and Christians stronger?

Contemplation

"Your rulers are rebels, companions of thieves; they all love bribes and chase after gifts" (Isaiah 1:23 NIV). Although Isaiah wrote to Judah, these words applied equally well to the Northern Kingdom of Israel and to Herod Agrippa I, who ruled for Rome. I marvel at how far away from God kings of Israel, Judah, and Judea moved. While marveling, I look at the government of my country and our allies and enemies. The same types of behavior that occurred two or three thousand years ago occur today. Do present leaders learn nothing from history? Surely, they can see what happens when nations turn from God, e.g., Israel, Judah, the Roman Empire.

Following God need not be a hit-or-miss process. God gave the Israelite kings and us a formula for following him. That formula is to read—and adhere—to God's words each day. Most of us won't be a king/queen, probably not even a president, a billionaire, or a minister of a megachurch. Nonetheless, God wants a successful relationship with us, and he wants our relationships with fellow Christians to be successful.

Pondering Ruling and Reigning Relationships

1. From these little known rulers' lives, we learn that when kings and citizens don't follow God, their lives are ruinous to themselves and to those who live under them. Is your behavior ruining anyone's life? If so, think about specific changes you can make.

2. Many of us grew up where Christianity was defined more by what we couldn't do than what we could do. What if, instead of being told not to do x, y, or z, we copied a book of the New Testament, e.g., Roman's, or Christ's Sermon on the Mount? Then, we carry this book or chapters with us (perhaps on an iPad). Daily we read all or part of it. Would we learn to revere God more? Would we better know how Christ expects us to live in relationship with others? Would our lives better reflect Christ?

Chapter 8

Governors

In biblical times, a governor was an administrator who acted on behalf of a king or emperor. He was the king's surrogate in the region. Governors didn't make basic policy, i.e., how much tax money to send to the king each year; however, a governor controlled how taxes would be collected in his region. Governors had great autonomy as long as they maintained peace and kept the money flowing to the king.

From the beginning of earth's time, God used governors. He created the sun to "govern" the day and the moon to "govern" the night (Genesis 1:16 NIV). As omniscient king, God knew the earth needed governors. He assigned subordinate governing roles to his creatures. For example, man to rule over animals.

The apostle Paul saw that some individuals had a gift for governance. He wrote that when individuals were given the spiritual gift of leadership, they should govern diligently, e.g., attentively, carefully, and thoroughly. Regretfully, not all governors were diligent. Job's young friend, Elihu, pondered, "Can he who hates justice govern?" (Job 34:17 NIV).

Just as God directed governors to rule diligently, he outlined responsibilities for people being governed. Christians are to obey governing authorities because God set them up. Whoever resists authority, resists what God appointed. Does that mean we are to obey a government action that violates scriptures? Of course not! Christians are to obey God rather than men. If a government violates biblical laws, Christians are obligated to disobey the government on the recognized issue.

In the Old Testament, God directed the Israelites to destroy idolatrous, perverted nations in the Promised Land. Technically, God established these governments. How could he then direct the Israelites to destroy them? The answer is that these Canaanite governments became ungodly; they no longer represented God.

We call political heads of states governors. The head of the United States government is called president. In reality, both United States state and federal heads are governors. Unlike kings or emperors, their authority is set by federal and state laws. Governors feel, or should feel, that they are responsible to constituents. When governors move from governing attentively, carefully, and thoroughly to manipulating truth and circumstances, they sin. While many well-intentioned politicians have redefined ethical expectations for governors, God has not. God expects moral behavior from civil and church governors.

As we encounter the six governors in this chapter, we see some who were just. They were men we can admire. In contrast, some governors acted deceitfully. They governed carelessly, and their correspondence showed that they were manipulators. They attacked Jews and Christians without cause. Over fifteen years ago, Barbara Hosbach (1989) wrote a book titled *Fools, Liars, Cheaters and Other Bible Heroes*. None of this chapter's six governors appeared in Hosbach's book; however, fools, liars, and cheats aptly describe two of them; hero applies to two, and the jury is still out on the remaining two. See how you categorize these six lesser-known Bible governors:

- Gedaliah, Nebuchadnezzar governor
- Zerubbabel, restoration governor
- Tattenai, impartial governor
- Rehum, manipulative governor
- Felix, unscrupulous governor
- Festus, inexperienced governor

Gedaliah, Nebuchadnezzar's Governor
(2 Kings 25:22–26; Jeremiah 40:7–41:10)

Heart of Story

Nebuchadnezzar appointed Gedaliah governor of Judea. He was murdered by a remaining member of Judah's royal family.

Story Line

After the Babylonians destroyed Jerusalem, Nebuchadnezzar appointed Gedaliah as territorial governor. He was a Jew, although not a member of the royal family. Gedaliah was well-educated and a political moderate. He organized the new capital at Mizpah, eight miles north of Jerusalem. Since the days of the judges, Mizpah was a place where Israelites went to worship God.

Gedaliah knew Judah was no longer an independent nation. He governed for Nebuchadnezzar. Babylonian soldiers were garrisoned at Mizpah. Gedaliah told the remaining Jews that they had nothing to fear if they remained in the country, farmed the land, and served Nebuchadnezzar.

The Babylonian commander sent King Zedekiah's daughters to Gedaliah. Jeremiah went to Mizpah to be near Gedaliah. Jews who fled to other countries during the Babylonian siege returned to Judah and Mizpah. Jewish army officers and soldiers not killed in the Babylonian War visited Mizpah. The first year Gedaliah was governor, the land yielded a large quantity of wine and summer fruit.

From the time the Israelites entered the Promised Land, the Ammonites warred against them. The Ammonite king, Baalis, hated the Jews. He sent Ishmael to kill Gedaliah. Ishmael was a member of Judah's royal family. A Judah army officer, Johanan, warned Gedaliah about Baalis's plan. Secretly, Johanan offered to kill Ishmael so Ishmael wouldn't kill Gedaliah and bring Babylonian reprisals on the Jews. Gedaliah dismissed Johanan's warning and ordered him not to kill Ishmael.

Shortly afterward, Ishmael and ten men came to Mizpah. Hospitably, Gedaliah served them a meal. While they were eating, Ishmael and his men killed Gedaliah, some Jews with him, and the Babylonian soldiers. The following day, Ishmael and his men slaughtered a group of men, who came to make a sacrifice at the Lord's house in Mizpah. Ishmael filled a cistern with the bodies of Gedaliah and the men he slaughtered. Ishmael took captive those Jews who remained at Mizpah and headed toward Ammon.

Pondering Relationships

Bible chronology and history indicate that Gedaliah governed anywhere from two months to several years (ESV). Everything recorded about Gedaliah indicated that he was humble and conciliatory. He wanted to shield Jews from further suffering. Gedaliah treated equally well poor Jews, who worked the land, and Judean military, who escaped Babylonian slaughter. He didn't gloat about his rank or power as governor. Instead, Gedaliah offered to represent the Jews to the Babylonians.

Gedaliah couldn't conceive of anyone, particularly a member of the royal family, plotting against him. Killing Gedaliah was tantamount to declaring war against Babylon. The Bible provides no rationale for Ishmael's behavior. Perhaps, he saw Gedaliah as a traitor to the Jewish people because Gedaliah governed for Nebuchadnezzar. As royalty, Ishmael's pride may have been wounded when Gedaliah, not he, was named governor.

My husband sees Gedeliah as an exceptional Jewish man who put his faith in God. Gedaliah trusted God to take care of him. He accepted God's will for his life, even if that meant he would be murdered. Bruce sees Old Testament Gedaliah as a foreshadow of Christ in the New Testament.

I see this point of view; however, Gedaliah reminds me of today's politicians who see the best in everyone and in every situation. What a wonderful trait, except when it causes blindness to reality. When Christ sent his apostles to teach and preach in the Galileen towns, he advised them to be as wise as serpents and innocent as doves. Gedaliah was an innocent dove; he couldn't believe that Ishmael would kill him. Perhaps, Gedaliah also needed to be wise as a serpent. Wisdom would have allowed Gedaliah to consider that Ishmael, who spent time in the Ammonite court, may have been influenced by the Ammonite king.

Reflection

Gedeliah built relationships with Babylonian conquerers and his many Jewish constituents. How do you build relationships with your constituents, e.g., spouse, children, colleagues at work, and at church?

Zerubbabel, Restoration Governor
(Ezra 1–4:5, 6:16–22)

Heart of the Story

Zerubbabel was the first governor of the Jews who returned from Babylon to Judea. He was an ancestor of Christ.

Story Line

When King Cyrus conquered Babylon (539 BC), he gave the Jews permission to return to Jerusalem. He ordered them to rebuild the temple to their god. Cyrus gave Sheshbazzar the original temple articles that Nebuchadnezzar carried into Babylon. Study Bibles and scholars equivocate on whether Sheshbazzar was the Persian name for Zerubbabel, or if the two were different men. The *New Strong's Exhaustive Concordance of the Bible* noted that Sheshbazzar was Zerubbabel's Chaldean name (Strong, 2010).

Zerubbabel was the first political leader of the approximately fifty thousand Jews who returned to Jerusalem (538–537 BC). These Jews were from three Israelite tribes: Judah, Benjamin, and Levi. Most were born in Babylon; only a very few lived in Judah as children. Although he is referred to as a governor, Zerubbabel's authority was limited to the Jews who returned with him.

About three months after Jews resettled in Judea, they met in Jerusalem. It was the seventh month, Tishri (roughly September–October). Zerubbabel and the chief priest, Jeshua, rebuilt the temple altar. Jewish priests offered burnt sacrifices on it. Jews celebrated the Festival of Tabernacles (Booths), which commemorated the Israelite's exodus from Egypt.

The following year, the foundation of the temple was laid. Construction began in the second month (Ziv). Solomon started construction of his temple in the same month. At that time, people, e.g., Samaritans, who lived in the region approached Zerubbabel. They offered to help build the temple, noting that they worshipped the same God as the returned exiles. After consulting the chief priest Jeshua, Zerubbabel declined their offer. He explained that King Cyrus commanded the returned exiles to rebuild the temple.

Offended by Zerubbabel's response, the Samaritans began to intimidate the builders. Their intimidation was so forceful that Jews were terrified to continue construction. Samaritans bribed Persian and even Jewish counselors to thwart rebuilding efforts. These harassments continued for about sixteen years. During this time, temple construction slowed (536–530 BC) and rebuilding ceased (530–520 BC) for about ten years.

In early autumn of 520 BC, the prophet Haggai received a message from God. God reprimanded the Jews for living in their paneled houses, while the temple, his home, remained in ruins. Immediately, Zerubbabel, Jeshua, and the Jewish remnant resumed temple construction. The second Jewish temple to God was completed and dedicated in 516/515 BC, twenty-two years after Cyrus allowed the Jewish exiles to return to Jerusalem.

Pondering Relationships

Often in Jewish history, tension existed between the civilian and ecclesiastical authorities. None of these tensions were identified during this twenty-plus-year period. Governor Zerubbabel and chief priest, Jeshua, acted in concert to restore the Jews to their homeland and rebuild the temple.

Zerubbabel refused to allow the Samaritans and people of the land to assist the Jews in construction of the temple. His refusal showed that God's people shouldn't always accept assistance from others, particularly when their beliefs and actions aren't consistent with belief in God. The Samaritan's help would have allowed temple construction to move faster; but, it would have had negative effects. The Samaritan worship of God was interwoven with worship of gods and goddesses from other countries. If Zerubbabel accepted their help, they would have a right to worship in the temple. From its inception, temple worship would be polluted by foreign beliefs, and possibly by idols.

I'm not sure why Zerubbabel allowed opponents to slow down and stop temple construction for sixteen years. True, the Jews were terrified of the Samaritans and other people who lived in the land; yet, surely, Zerubbabel realized that God was more powerful than any opponent. Zerubbabel's reaction mirrored that of the first generation of Israelites who fled Egypt. They knew only a life of slavery. They didn't believe they could conquer the Promised Land. Initially, Zerubbabel may have doubted that God planned for the exiles to rebuild the temple.

For their first twenty years in Judea, the returned Jews didn't have a prophet, who spoke God's message to them. Even though he was the political leader, Zerubbabel needed to be aroused by Haggai's words and encouraged by Zechariah's visions. To Zerubbabel, a prophet in their midst meant God favored the restored Jews and still spoke directly to them.

Reflection

Why didn't Zerubbabel move forward with temple construction as soon as the Jews returned to Jerusalem? Is fear a reason not to undertake a project for God?

Tattenai, Impartial Governor
(Ezra 5–6)

Heart of the Story

Governor Tattenai allowed the Jews to continue building God's temple while he investigated whether or not King Cyrus gave them permission to build it.

Story Line

The events in this story (Ezra 5 and 6) occurred between 520–516/515 BC. Tattenai was the Persian governor of "Beyond the River" province, where Judea was located. Persian records showed that Tattenai reported to Ushtannu (Hystanes), who was the overall governor or satrap of the Trans-Euphrates region.

At the beginning of King Darius I's reign, revolts flared throughout the Persian Empire. In this volatile environment, Governor Tattenai got word that the Jews were rebuilding their temple. Probably, groups who discouraged and frustrated temple building a decade earlier apprised Tattenai of the Jew's activity. As governor, Tattenai needed to ensure that resumption of temple construction wasn't, or didn't evolve into, another revolt. He went to Jerusalem to investigate.

When Governor Tattenai met with the Jewish leaders, he asked them two questions: (a) who gave you a decree to build the temple, and (b) what are the names of the men who are doing the building? Using information from the Jewish leaders, Tattenai wrote a letter to King Darius I and asked the king to verify the Jew's account.

Darius I ordered a search of King Cyrus's records to find a decree that Cyrus ordered the temple to be rebuilt. Although Cyrus's actual decree wasn't found, a scroll mentioning the decree was found in Cyrus summer palace at Ecbatana. The Jews were correct—King Cyrus gave Jews permission to return to Jerusalem, build a temple to God, and place the gold and silver vessels in it.

King Darius I ordered Governor Tattenai and his officials to let the Jews build their god's temple and to pay the costs from the royal treasury. Tattenai was to provide the Jewish priests with animals, wine, oil, etc., for daily temple sacrifices. In return, the Jews were to pray for the lives of the king and his sons when they made daily sacrifices. In his letter to Tattenai, King Darius I ordered that if anyone altered his edict, the person was to be killed and his house destroyed.

Ezra recorded that Tattenai followed King Darius I's orders diligently. In four to five years, the Jews finished construction of the second temple in Jerusalem. The second temple was finished almost seventy years after the destruction of Solomon's temple.

Pondering Relationships

Tattenai's behavior in Ezra 5 and 6 depicted an impartial Persian governor. Although he heard gossip about the rebellious history of the Jews, Tattenai didn't rush to judgment. He investigated the Jerusalem temple construction firsthand. Probably, Tattenai resided in Samaria about thirty-five miles north of Jerusalem; however, his seat of government could have been Damascus, a full 135 miles north of Jerusalem. Either way, traveling to Jerusalem was costly and inconvenient for him.

Paul wrote that rulers/governors hold no terror for individuals who do right and commended these individuals. When Governor Tattenai asked Jewish leaders why they were rebuilding the temple, they weren't afraid. Ultimately, Tattenai commended both Zerubbabel and Joshua for temple construction by supplying them with money from the royal treasury.

When Tattenai heard the Jew's explanation for building the temple, he didn't order them to stop construction until he heard back from King Darius I. He assumed that the Jews were telling the truth. Possibly, he concluded that each people craved a place where they could worship their god.

Tattenai asked the Jews for the names of the men who were building the temple. His motivation could have been to differentiate these men from the remainder of the Jewish population. If King Darius I ordered temple construction to stop and builders punished, Tattenai knew exactly who to punish. He wouldn't indiscriminately arrest or kill innocent men.

Tattenai's letter to King Darius I noticeably lacked any personal opinion or bias. He reported exactly what he observed. Then, he asked for information from the king. His letter to King Darius I gave the impression that he was a willing servant of the empire. He would act in any way the king directed.

Conceivably, Darius I's response reduced Tattenai's personal income. Nonetheless, Tattenai enacted Darius I's directions meticulously. Although the Bible doesn't document what happened to Tattenai, historical documents recorded that he was later promoted to satrap of the entire Trans-Euphrates region (Ushtannu's position).

Reflection

The writer of the book of Ezra respected Tattenai. Do you think that Tattenai was pro-Jewish, or just evenhanded? What characteristics of Tattenai contributed to his later promotion?

Rehum, Manipulative Governor
(Ezra 4; Nehemiah 1, 2:1–10)

Heart of the Story

Governor Rehum didn't want the Jews to have the security of a wall around Jerusalem. He manipulated King Artaxerxes I into supporting his position.

Story Line

During the reigns of Persian Kings Xerxes I (485–465 BC) and Artaxerxes I (465–424 BC), officials in the Trans-Euphrates satrapy thwarted Jews from rebuilding Jerusalem's protective wall. One official was Rehum, identified in Ezra 4 as a commanding officer. Rehum wasn't a military officer but a high government official, i.e., governor. Probably, he lived in Samaria. The Bible narrative of Rehum is sandwiched between Ezra 4:5 and Ezra 4:24. Chronologically, Rehum's actions fit in the initial chapters of Nehemiah or as background to Nehemiah.

For ancient civilizations, a city wall had physical and psychological importance. Physically, the wall protected citizens from invading armies and prevented robbers and cutthroats from troubling residents. Psychologically, the wall was a source of security and pride. Ancient records often described the height and width of a city's wall. Not having a city wall was an embarrassment to residents. Its absence indicated extreme poverty, laziness, or indifference to human life.

Rehum's letter to King Artaxerxes I began with a description of governors, officials, and groups who were in agreement with it. The men's high ranks and the array of nationalities would have impressed King Artaxerxes I. He didn't know the history between the Jews and some coalition members. For example, the Elamites were century-old enemies of the Jews, who missed no opportunity to undermine Jewish lives and well-being.

The letter's thrust was that the Jews were rebuilding Jerusalem, which Rehum called a rebellious and wicked city. The official letter concluded that once Jerusalem was rebuilt, the Jews would no longer pay tribute, custom, and toll. Royal revenue from the area would dry up. Rehum assured King Artaxerxes I that he and his colleagues were writing only because they were loyal. They didn't want to see the king dishonored.

Rehum requested that Persian archives be searched to verify that Jerusalem was destroyed because it was a rebellious city. He concluded with the dire warning that if the Jerusalem walls were built, the king would have nothing left west of the Euphrates River.

At this time, the western Persian Empire was in turmoil. Artaxerxes I put down an Egyptian revolt in 459 BC and a revolt by the satrap (Megabysus) of "Beyond the River" around 448 BC (Rainey, 1969). Given these revolts, King Artaxerxes I was sensitive to any hint of rebellion in his western province. Governor Rehum's suggestion that the Jews were fermenting a rebellion got King Artaxerxes I's immediate attention.

King Artaxerxes I had the royal archives searched. He found that Rehum was correct. Jerusalem was a place of rebellion and sedition. In a return letter, King Artaxerxes I ordered Rehum to stop the Jews from further construction in Jerusalem. His letter was emphatic—the Jewish threat to Persia shouldn't be allowed to grow. Rehum went to Jerusalem and compelled the Jews to stop rebuilding Jerusalem, to include the city walls. Rehum may have destroyed some structures and walls that were rebuilt by Jews who lived there.

Pondering Relationships

Little is known about Governor Rehum in either Bible or historical literature. *Rehum* was a common Jewish and Aramaic name in the Persian Empire. Despite being a governor for the Persian Empire, Rehum may not have been Persian. His letter was written in Aramaic, rather than in the Persian language.

Governor Rehum manipulated the truth and played on King Artaxerxes I's fear of rebellion. Fewer than one hundred thousand Jews lived in the tiny Judean province. Most were famers and small-time craftsmen with families. The Jews didn't have a standing army. They couldn't challenge the might of Persia. Rehum's claim that if the Jews rebuilt the Jerusalem walls, Persia would have no revenue from the immense Trans-Euphrates satrapy was an overstatement.

The coalition of important men, regions, and nationalities who sent the letter to Artaxerxes was substantial. Seemingly, there was no Jewish representative or diplomat in Rehum's court to explain why Jews wanted a wall around Jerusalem. The returned exiles didn't recognize the importance of building alliances or having representation in other national courts.

When Rehum's behavior and letter to King Artaxerxes I are compared to Tattenai's to King Darius I, the differences are noteworthy. Rehum didn't go to Jerusalem to learn firsthand what the Jews were doing or wanted to do. Rehum already made up his mind about the motives and future activities of the Jews. In contrast, Tattenai reported only what he observed and heard. Further, Rehum told King Artaxerxes I what to look for in the archives, i.e., Jerusalem was a rebellious city, to confirm his conclusions. In contrast, Tattenai asked for archival information to clarify and verify the Jewish situation. Rehum revealed himself as an alarmist with an anti-Semitic agenda.

Reflection

How did Reham's rush-to-rush judgment about Jewish motives hurt his relationship with the Jews and possibly with Artaxerxes I? Who would you prefer to govern you: Tattenai or Rehum?

Felix, Inexperienced Governor
(Acts 24)

Heart of the Story

Felix had the disposition of a slave and the power of a tyrant. He listened to Paul's witness about Christ in the hope that Paul would offer him a bribe.

Story Line

Marcus Antonius Felix was the Roman governor of Judea (65–59/60 BC) when Paul was accused of creating a revolt in the Jerusalem temple. Felix lived in Caesarea Maritima, about seventy miles north of Jerusalem.

According to Josephus, Jewish affairs deteriorated during Felix's governorship (Whiston, 1987). The country was filled with robbers and impostors who deluded the people. Felix used deception to capture some criminals, which caused the Judean populace to mistrust him. Jonathan, a Jewish high priest instrumental in securing Felix's appointment as governor, reproved Felix about the way he governed. In response, Felix had him killed.

In fairness, Felix had little experience as a governor when he attained his position. He was born a slave, became a freedman, then a high government official. Felix's brother, Pallans, was Claudius's favorite minister. Pallan obtained the governorship for Felix. In succession, Felix married three royal ladies. While Judea's governor, he fell in love with the beautiful Drusilla, the daughter of King Herod Agrippa I. She was the wife of Azizus, king of Emesa. Drusilla divorced Azizus and married Felix.

To protect Paul from the Jerusalem Jewish leaders, Commander Claudius Lysias delivered Paul to Governor Felix in Caesarea Maritima. Five days later, Jews arrived in Felix's court to present their case against Paul. The Jewish contingent included Ananias, high priest of the Jerusalem temple, and Tertullus, a well-known prosecuting attorney.

When Tertullus presented the Jew's case against Paul, he began with overblown flattery. He identified that Felix brought peace to the land, and his foresight brought reforms to the nation. Then, Tertullus listed four distinct charges against Paul. Paul:

- Was a plague, i.e., a pest, nuisance.
- Created a revolt among Jews.
- Was a ringleader of the Nazarene sect.
- Tried to profane the temple.

Felix allowed Paul to respond to the accusations. Paul pointed out that he arrived in Jerusalem to worship only twelve days before he was arrested. In that short time, he couldn't have become a nuisance. When his accusers accosted him, no one was with Paul. He wasn't arguing with anyone; therefore, he couldn't have caused a temple riot. Paul admitted that he followed "The Way" (early name for Christianity), which included the belief that there would be a resurrection. Paul recounted that he brought offerings and gifts for the Jerusalem poor.

Pondering Relationships

Felix was in a difficult situation. He didn't want to offend the illustrious Jewish contingent; yet, Paul, a Roman citizen, didn't break Roman law. Like many judiciaries caught in a perceived no-win situation, Felix postponed his decision. He said that after Commander Claudius Lysias came from Jerusalem and testified, he would rule on Paul's case. Felix ordered a military officer to keep Paul under guard; but, he gave Paul some freedom and permitted friends to take care of Paul's needs.

Paul's trial before Felix occurred two years before Felix was recalled to Rome to account for his rule. In the two years, Claudius Lysias didn't appear before Felix to testify in Paul's case. Periodically, Felix brought Paul to him in hope that Paul would offer him a bribe to secure his freedom. Felix wanted to free Paul, but wanted money for doing so.

For this Roman governor, who had little morality as a man or as a leader, Paul's words were convicting. While Felix and Drusilla listened to Paul's discourse on righteousness, self-control, and judgment, Felix became frightened. He told Paul, "That's enough for now! You may leave. When I find it convenient, I will send for you" (Acts 24:25 NIV). Felix's fear demonstrated that he correctly doubted whether his actions were right with God, i.e., he was self-controlled and his judgments just.

Reflection

Both the Jewish priest, Jonathan, and Paul provided Felix with wise instruction. However, Felix discounted their words and ruled by guile and greed. Ponder why Felix, government officials today, and you don't accept wise counsel. How does accepting counsel enhance relationships?

Festus, Unscrupulous Governor
(Acts 25)

Heart of the Story

Very soon after becoming governor of Judea, Festus heard Paul's case. When Festus pushed Paul to return to Jerusalem for trial by the Sanhedrin, Paul demanded a hearing before Caesar.

Story Line

When Emperor Nero called Felix to Rome in AD 62, Porcius Festus became governor of Judea. Three days after arriving in Caesarea, he went to Jerusalem to meet with Jewish leaders. By then, a full two years had passed since Governor Felix refused to indite Paul for profaning the temple. Despite the two years, the Jerusalem Jews didn't forget Paul. They asked Festus to return Paul to Jerusalem to stand trial in front of the Sanhedrin. Instead of agreeing to their request, Festus invited the Jews to present their case against Paul in his court in Caesarea.

When Paul was brought before the Roman civil court in Caesarea, three groups were present. The first was Festus and his council. The second was Jews from Jerusalem, who brought charges against Paul. Finally, Paul was present to answer charges and present a defense.

Neither the Jew's accusations nor Paul's defense were outlined in Acts chapter 25. Likely, they mirrored those outlined in Acts chapter 24. The outcome was that Festus—wishing to do the Jews a favor—asked Paul if he was willing to go to Jerusalem and stand trial. Essentially, Paul's response was "Of course not." As a Roman citizen, Paul had the right to a trial in a Roman court, where he was currently standing. To prevent Festus from remanding him to the Jewish Sanhedrin, Paul appealed his case to Caesar.

Appeal to Caesar was the right of every Roman citizen. The appeal mirrors one to the United States Supreme Court. Roman law required that the lower court write an explicit report on the case when it was sent to Caesar. Regional governors weren't permitted to send petty cases to the emperor; however, once a Roman citizen appealed to Caesar, Roman courts and Roman officials were required to implement the appeal.

Pondering Relationships

When Festus assumed the governorship of Judea, he had to secure peace and to reduce Jew's bitter feelings toward Rome. Festus knew that Jewish complaints were a reason Governor Felix was recalled to Rome. To calm the aggressive populace, Festus needed the goodwill of the Jewish religious leaders.

A challenge for Festus was that the Jews believed that they had special privilege or entitlement associated with their religion. The special privilege meant that Jews could pass religious laws and hold court to enforce them. In Paul's case, Jewish ecclesiastical law butted heads with laws of Roman citizenship that Festus had to enforce.

Any decision made by Caesar overturned lower court rulings. Caesar could acquit Paul of charges of breaking Jewish law. Importantly, Caesar's ruling in Paul's favor would recognize that Christianity wasn't a Jewish sect, subject to Jewish laws, but a religion distinct from Judaism. Such a distinction would curtail future Jewish intrusion into the Christian religion.

At first consideration, Governor Festus appears disingenuous when he asked Paul if he was willing to return to Jerusalem to stand trial before the Sanhedrin. Logically, Paul was going to say "No." Festus's continued push at Paul to agree to return to Jerusalem almost guaranteed that Paul would appeal to Caesar.

With Paul's appeal, Festus moved from a no-win situation to a "my hands are tied" one. Likely, Festus gave a huge sigh of relief. By Roman law, Festus had to send Paul to Caesar. Paul's appeal to Caesar mandated that Festus refuse to send him to the Sanhedrin for judgment and prevented Jewish leaders from blaming Festus for the decision.

Reflection

How did the outcome of Paul's hearing before Festus strengthen Festus's relationship with the Jewish leaders?

Contemplation

The great poet and essayist Ralph Waldo Emerson (1803–1882) concluded that "The punishment which the wise suffer who refuse to take part in the government, is to live under the government of worse men" (Esar, 1968). Certainly, the governor narratives in this chapter demonstrated the moral imperative for Christian men and women to become active in politics and government.

All bad government cannot be prevented by Christian involvement; however, no or little participation from Christians almost guarantees problematic government. Once elected to political office, Christian politicians can't allow expediency and need for reelection to take precedence over implementing God's standards.

Governor Relationships

1. Zerubbabel was the grandson of a king; yet, he was content to be governor of the small province of Judea under Babylon. Likely, he expended effort to accommodate Jeshua, the chief priest. How could a king's grandson be so adaptable? Do you think Zerubbabel understood that he was going to be an ancestor of the Messiah? Why or why not?

2. How did the returned Jewish exiles hurt their cause by not having representation in courts of local and regional governers? Would

a Jewish presence in Rehum's court have diminished some of Rehum's hostility toward the Jews?

3. How were Governors Felix and Festus similar and different? Describe each governor's relationship with Jewish leaders. Be sure to review how each acted toward Paul, the man Jewish leaders tried to kill.

CHAPTER 9

Military Officers

Biblical military officers had responsibility for and authority over soldiers who served under them. They obeyed military officers higher in their chain of command and certain civilian authorities. An example is the Roman commander (tribune) assigned to Jerusalem, Judea during Christ's ministry. He obeyed both his Legion commander and Pilate, the Roman governor of Judea. Obedience implies compliance with the commands or orders of an individual in authority. In the ancient Near East, when a man accepted sanctuary in a country, he had an obligation for military service to that country.

In the Old Testament, over twelve words were used to describe military leaders. Recently, Bibles translated most of these words as commander or captain. Usually, a commander had broad responsibility for military forces, i.e., commander of pharaoh's army or King David's army; however, sometimes commander referred to an officer with more circumscribed duties, i.e., Nebuzaradan, commander of the Babylonian imperial guard.

Typically, a captain led a smaller cadre of men than a commander. He obeyed his commander's orders. The size of a captain's unit varied. Isaiah referred to a captain with about fifty men at his command. In contrast, King Achish of Gath made David captain of his bodyguard for life. At the time, David had six hundred fighting men under his command.

Before the Israelites entered the Promised Land, Moses identified that officers should exempt the following men from battle or war (Deuteronomy 20:5–9). Men who:

- Built a new house but didn't live in it.

- Planted a vineyard but didn't yet enjoy its fruits.

- Were pledged to a woman but not yet married to her.

- Were afraid or fainthearted about an upcoming battle or war.

In the New Testament, Roman military used the title *centurion* in addition to commander or captain. Centurions had about one hundred men under them. Some were infantry officers while others headed cavalry units. Frequently, Roman commanders had both infantry and cavalry units among their troops. Although it is difficult to compare the rank of a centurion with a rank in the US Army, centurion sounds like a first or second lieutenant who led from the front.

When soldiers came to John to be baptized, they asked him what they should do (Luke 3:14). John replied that soldiers shouldn't extort money or falsely accuse people. Soldiers should be content with their pay. Paul recognized that soldiers endured hardship (2 Timothy 2:3–4). He observed that a good soldier doesn't get involved in civilian affairs; rather, he obeys his commanding officer.

The following six stories of lesser known military officers represent commanders, captains, and centurions. Four were from the Old Testament and two were New Testament Roman military officers. No effort was made to choose good over not-so-good officers; however, all six were remarkably competent. Most cared for their men and implemented orders. Only one was an inexperienced military leader; however, he had God's support so experience wasn't a factor in his success:

- Barak, reluctant commander

- Ittai, loyal Philistine commander

- Nebuzaradan, career Babylonian commander

- Johanan, fearful captain

- Claudius Lysias, Roman tribune

- Julius, upright centurion

Barak, Reluctant Commander
(Judges 4)

Heart of the Story

Barak was unprepared to be the war commander of Israel against the Canaanites. His victory was due to God's plan, not his skill.

Story Line

King Jabin ruled from Hazor, a well-fortified city in west-central Naphtali. He led a confederacy of Canaanite city-states that spread as far south as Ephraim. Life in rural villages almost ceased during the twenty-year period that King Jabin oppressed the Israelites. Villagers retreated to walled towns for protection. Sisera was Jabin's war commander. Sisera's well-supplied army included nine hundred iron chariots. His home was in southeast Asher.

Deborah was the fourth judge after the Israelites entered the Promised Land. She held court under a palm tree in the southern hill country of Ephraim. When the Israelites repented of their idol worship and cried to God for relief from Jabin's oppression, God responded. He instructed Deborah to send for Barak, an Israelite from northern Naphtali. Deborah told Barak that God wanted him to lead the Israelites to defeat Sisera's army.

Barak was reluctant to accept the commander's role. He would only agree if Deborah accompanied the Israelite army. Deborah wasn't happy with Barak's response. She told Barak that because he mandated her presence, God would give credit for killing Sisera to a woman, rather than to Barak.

Barak gathered the Israelite troops on Mount Tabor in the Jazreel Valley. God lured Sisera to the valley by allowing him to learn that the Israelite army was camped there. Sisera was confident that he could defeat the Israelites. The flat Jazreel Valley was an ideal place to maximize the advantage of fast chariots against Israelite foot soldiers. Sisera made no plan to defeat the Israelites without his chariots.

The Kishon River passed through the Jazreel Valley. God caused a heavy rain. The Kishon River flooded, creating a marsh on both sides of the river. Sisera's chariots couldn't maneuver in the mud. Israelite soldiers killed the Canaanite troops. Sisera abandoned his chariot and fled on foot.

When Sisera neared his home in Ashur, he came to tents belonging to Heber, a Kenite. Believing the Kenites were allies, he entered the camp. Sisera accepted milk from Heber's wife, Jael and fell asleep in her tent. Jael killed Sisera by driving a tent peg through his temple. Shortly afterward, Barak came to the Kenite camp. Jael showed him Sisera's dead body.

Pondering Relationships

From an earthly perspective, Barak's willingness to command the Israelite army is remarkable for three reasons. First, over 250 years had passed since the Israelites entered the Promised Land. Barak had little more than legend to credit that God cared for his people. It was going to take divine intervention for the Israelites to win a battle against Sisera and his seasoned army. Second, Deborah held court approximately eighty miles from Barak's hometown. Barak may have known Deborah only by reputation. Initially, he wasn't sure Deborah spoke for God rather than herself. Third, Barak was from a small clan in one of the lesser known tribes of Israel. He had no experience with military command.

Can you imagine Barak sending home some Israelite man who volunteered to fight in his army? Did he remember God's command to exempt certain men from war or battle? I think Barak obeyed God meticulously, knowing that the battle would be won by God, not by the number of Israelite troops. Ten thousand Israelite soldiers followed Commander Barak to Mount Tabor. Initially, there may have been more than ten thousand volunteers.

The multiple debits in Barak's abilities to command an army didn't matter. What mattered was Barak's faith that God would deliver the Canaanite army into Israelite hands. Barak's faith allowed him to conquer a kingdom. He is listed in the Hebrew Hall of Faith (Hebrews 11:32).

Reflection

Barak's initial response showed that he focused on Sisera's strength rather than on God's power. Analyze how Barak's relationship with Deborah and God evolved throughout his story.

Ittai, Loyal Philistine Commander
(I Samuel 27:1–7; 2 Samuel 15:13–23, 18:1–18, 21:20–22)

Heart of the Story

Loyal Ittai helped David survive a civil war. He was commander in a battle in which David's forces were outnumbered ten to one.

Story Line

When David was twenty-nine to thirty years of age, he lived in Gath, a major Philistine region. King Achish of Gath gave David the town of Ziklag. Along with six hundred soldiers and their families, David remained there for about sixteen months. Approximately, thirty years later, Prince Absalom led a rebellion against King David. David fled Jerusalem with palace guards and his personal bodyguards. These guards were Philistines.

In ancient times, it was usual for a king to employ foreign soldiers for his personal bodyguard. Soldiers from his own kingdom had regional or tribal loyalties that could compromise their allegiance to the king. The day before King David left Jerusalem, a group of Gath mercenaries arrived in Jerusalem. The group was composed of their leader, Ittai, six hundred fighting men, and their families. They came to be part of David's personal and palace guards.

King David led the exodus from Jerusalem. Some distance from the city, David halted and allowed followers to march past him. When he saw the Gittite soldiers and their families, David stopped Ittai. David suggested that Ittai go back to Jerusalem and stay with King Absalom. The Gittites only arrived in Jerusalem the day before David left the city. Why should the new arrivals undertake the hardship of going into exile with him?

Ittai's response was reminiscent of Ruth to Naomi when Naomi tried to send Ruth back to her people. Ittai averred, "As surely as the Lord lives, and as my lord the king lives, wherever my lord the king may be, whether it means life or death, there will your servant be" (2 Samuel 15:21 NIV).

In this dark hour when family members, trusted counselors, and even members of his tribe deserted David, a foreigner declared his loyalty. Ittai was willing to put his life, and lives of his men, and their families in peril for David. David could hardly speak; he said simply, "Go ahead, march on" (2 Samuel 15:22 NIV). David remained there while Ittai, soldiers, and their families went forward. David put himself between Ittai's company and any armed pursuit from Jerusalem.

Absalom assembled an estimated forty thousand troops. The army marched east across the Jordan River to confront King David's army. According to Josephus, David had about four thousand fighting men (Whiston, 1987). Determined to attack the Israelite army where the terrain would give his men maximum advantage, David sent out his troops: one-third under the command of Joab, one-third under the command of Abishai (Joab's brother), and one-third under the command of Ittai.

David's small army attacked the massive Israelite army in the forest of Ephraim. Different from a forest with tall trees, the Ephriam forest (Hebrew word ya'ar) was rough country, abounding in rocks, stones, and shurbs, and with only occasional trees. The battle spread over the whole countryside. Absalom and twenty thousand Israelite soldiers were killed. The Bible asserted that the forest claimed more lives that day than the sword.

Pondering Relationships

It makes sense that Ittai went to King David for work when he was exiled from Gath. David was the strongest regent living in proximity to Gath. Further, David acted honorably when he lived in Gath. Ittai, or some of his clan elders, may have remembered Captain David from thirty years earlier.

Have you ever wondered what Ittai and his men did to be exiled from Gath? He was a man of principle, an experienced commander, and had six hundred seasoned fighters at his command. Why would the Philistines expel such a valuable asset? Perhaps, the answer is as simple as God knew David needed Ittai, who viewed loyalty the same way David did.

Ittai's name provides insight into his personality. Ittai meant "with me." Ittai made a decision—in this case to support King David—and stuck with it. He was with David regardless of what and where David was, i.e., a king in a plush palace in Jerusalem or a deposed ruler in a country town. I wonder if David took consolation from having "with me" with him.

Ittai was a loyal but canny leader. Along with Joab and Abishai, Ittai recommended that David remain within the walls of Mahanaim during their attack on Absalom's force. Ittai was unwilling to compromise David's life or compromise the battle by allowing David's presence on the battlefield. He knew that if David was killed, his soldiers would have no reason to fight.

Some scholars suggested that David appointed Ittai as a commander because Ittai's men wouldn't fight under an Israelite commander. Others proposed that Joab and Abishai didn't trust the Philistines to be part of their forces. Although these arguments have validity, an alternative viewpoint is that David made Ittai a commander because he recognized Ittai's loyalty. David knew that Joab and Abishai would kill Prince Absalom if they had the chance. If Ittai captured Prince Absalom, his son's life would be spared.

The last time the Bible mentions Ittai is at the battle of the forest of Ephraim. Probably, he returned to Jerusalem with David and was integrated into David's palace guard. David was known for remembering loyal friends.

Reflection

Think about characteristics of a commander or leader you would follow on the battlefield.

Nebuzaradan, Career Babylonian Commander
(2 Kings 25:8–21; Jeremiah 39:8–14,
40:1–6, 52:12–15)

Heart of the Story

Nebuzaradan, the commander of Nebuchadnezzar's imperial guard, was given the assignment of destroying Jerusalem and rescuing Jeremiah.

Story Line

In 587 BC, Nebuchadnezzar routed King Zedekiah from Jerusalem. Shortly afterward, Zedekiah and his sons were killed. Nebuchadnezzar assigned Nebuzaradan, the commander of his imperial guard, the job of destroying Jerusalem. On August 14, 586 BC, Nebuzaradan arrived in Jerusalem. He set fire to Solomon's temple and the royal palace. Every important building in Jerusalem was burned down. The imperial guard broke down the Jerusalem walls and looted the city.

Nebuzaradan took senior temple priests and government officials to King Nebuchadnezzar in Riblah, where they were executed. Jews who defected to the Babylonians and some who remained in Jerusalem during the siege were taken to Babylon as captives. Only the poorest people were allowed to remain in Judah. These individuals were deemed powerless; therefore, would not incite rebellion. Nebuzaradan gave them vineyards and fields.

Nebuchadnezzar ordered Nebuzaradan to free Jeremiah and do whatever Jeremiah asked of him. Babylonian military leaders found Jeremiah in the courtyards of the guards. They sent Jeremiah to Gedaliah, the Nebuchadnezzar-appointed governor of Judea. Apparently, a mix-up occurred. Somehow, Jeremiah was swept up with other Jews, shackled, and started in a captive train to Babylon. Nebuzaradan found Jeremiah at Ramah (five miles north of Jerusalem) and released him.

Pondering Relationships

Nebuzaradan was the commander of the Babylonian imperial guard, an elite cohort of soldiers, answerable only to King Nebuchadnezzar. He was one of the greatest commanders of his day.

Nebuzaradan was less brutal than many other commanders in Nebuchadnezzar's army. Probably, when Jerusalem was sacked, Nebuzaradan remained at Riblah as bodyguard to Nebuchadnezzar. When Nebuchadnezzar sent Nebuzaradan to Jerusalem, his purpose was to destroy Jerusalem's buildings and walls. A brutal commander would have treated the remaining Jerusalemites as slaves and made them tear down the city's buildings and walls. Instead, Nebuzaradan used the Babylonian army to raze Jerusalem's structures.

Somehow, Nebuzaradan knew Jeremiah's prophecy that Babylon would overrun Jerusalem. He told Jeremiah, "The Lord your God decreed this disaster" and "All of this happened because you people sinned against the Lord and did not obey him" (Jeremiah 40:2-3 NIV). A Babylonian commander believed God's words given through Jeremiah, when Judah's leaders ignored them.

Nebuzaradan went the second mile to care for Jeremiah. Initially, he freed Jeremiah from confinement in the palace courtyard. Later, Nebuzaradan retrieved Jeremiah from a captive train headed for Babylon. Nebuzaradan even offered to take Jeremiah with him to Babylon. In Babylon, he would look after Jeremiah. Alternatively, Nebuzaraden said Jeremiah could go anywhere in the country. Consistent with Jeremiah's wishes, Nebuzaradan resent Jeremiah to Gedaliah. He also gave Jeremiah provisions and a present. Likely, Nebuzaradan gave Jeremiah written documentation of freedom to travel so Jeremiah wouldn't again be swept into a captive train.

Reflection

Nebuzaradan was an obedient and successful Babylonian war commander. Nebuchadnezzar valued him. What do you think his relationships with soldiers, captives, and enemies were like?

Johanan, Fearful Captain
(Jeremiah 40:8, 13–16, 41–43)

Heart of the Story

Gedaliah disregarded Johanan's warning that a member of the Jewish royal family planned to murder him. After Gedaliah was murdered, Johanan lead survivors to Egypt.

Story Line

In 596 BC, the Babylonians destroyed Jerusalem, killed King Zedekiah, and made Gedaliah governor of Judea. Most of the Jewish royal family was killed, but Ishmael, the son of Nethaniah and grandson of Elishama, remained alive. Soon after Gedaliah was appointed governor, Ishmael and King Baalis of Ammon plotted to kill him.

A former military captian, Johanan, and some of his soldiers, remained in the Judean countryside. He and other officers warned Gedaliah about Ishmael's plot. Johanan offered to kill Ishmael. He contended that if Gedaliah was murdered, the Jewish remnant would scatter and perish. Gedaliah refused to believe Johanan's accusation against Ishmael.

Later, Ishmael and his men not only killed Gedaliah but the Babylonian soldiers with him. Ishmael captured the remaining Jews under Gedaliah's care and started toward Ammon. When Johanan and his men heard what happened, they hurried after Absalom and the captives. At the pool of Gibeon, they caught up with Ishmael. In a subsequent fight, two of Ishmael's ten men were killed. Ishmael and the remainder fled to Ammon. The relieved captives joined Johanan.

Johanan was left to deal with the aftermath of Gedaliah's murder. Stressed and scared, Johanan halted near Bethlehem and turned to Jeremiah. Amazingly, the faithful prophet was still among the Mizpah refugees. Johanan and the Jews promised Jeremiah that if he asked God what they should do, they would follow God's direction. Jeremiah took their question to God. After ten days, God answered: the Jews should remain in Judea. In Judea, God would keep them safe. If they went to Egypt, they would die by sword, famine, and pestilence.

Johanan and Jewish leaders responded that Jeremiah was lying—God never said that they shouldn't go to Egypt! For some reason, the men accused Jeremiah's scribe, Baruch, of influencing Jeremiah to hand them over to the Babylonians. Then, Johanan and other military officers took the Jewish remnant to Egypt. They forced Jeremiah to go with them.

Pondering Relationships

When the Bible first portrayed Johanan, he seemed honorable, even likeable. He supported Gedaliah and cared about the Jewish remnant. He offered to kill Gedaliah's enemy, who was in league with the Ammonite king. When Johanan learned that Ishmael killed Gedaliah and took Jews captive, he hurried to free them.

Something changed in Johanan. Maybe it was the realization that he was no longer responsible only for himself and his battle-hardened soldiers. Now, helpless men, women, and children depended on him. How could he keep them safe? Where could he get them food, clothing, and shelter? We can almost see Johanan's stomach tightening as he realized the extent of his responsibility.

Johanan didn't want to go to Egypt. Even though the Israelite exodus from Egypt was nine hundred years earlier, Egypt stuck in Israelite's craw. Psalmists, sages, and prophets told stories about the horrific years the Israelites lived there as slaves. On the other hand, Egypt remained one of the few countries not conquered by the Babylonians. It was the breadbasket of the ancient Middle East. The Jewish remnant greatly feared famine and starvation. Many had lived through the siege of Jerusalem.

Johanan weighed his inclination to avoid Egypt and Jeremiah's words against his responsibility to care for the Jews with him. He decided to play it safe (in his own mind) and take the Jews to Egypt. Johanan disregarded God's words spoken through Jeremiah, despite having ample evidence that Jeremiah spoke for God.

After Johanan rejected Jeremiah's message, the Bible recorded no information about him. A few years later, Pharaoh Hophra was assassinated. Nebuchadnezzar took advantage of the political upheaval, invaded Egypt, and conquered it. Most of the Jewish refugees in Egypt perished. Probably, Johanan was killed. Hopefully, he died as a soldier fighting for the lives of his people.

Reflection

How do you think Johannan felt about the Jewish remnant in his care? Do you think he ever wanted to simply abandon them and go his own way? Ponder how fear drives our actions in relationships.

Claudius Lysias, Roman Tribune
(Acts 23)

Heart of the Story

Commander Lysias rescued Paul from almost certain death by a Jewish mob. He investigated the reason for the Jew's animosity while protecting Paul.

Story Line

Claudius Lysias was the commander (tribune) of the Roman soldiers garrisoned at the Tower of Antonio. These barracks were adjacent to the Jerusalem temple. Commander Lysias led a cohort, or one-tenth of a Roman Legion; thus, he commanded between six hundred to one thousand men that included foot soldiers and cavalry. He was a Roman citizen who bought his citizenship at a high price. In the middle of the first century, the Jerusalem temple was the center of the Jewish rebel movement against Rome.

Paul was a Roman citizen, Jew, and Christian. He was in Jerusalem to celebrate the seven-day festival of Pentecost (*Shau'ot*, Festival of Weeks). While undergoing purification in the temple, Paul was attacked by a mob. The mob claimed Paul taught against the Mosaic law and defiled the temple by bringing a Greek into it. Members of the mob seized Paul, dragged him from the temple, and attempted to kill him.

Hearing the uproar, Claudius Lysias left the Antonio Fortress, ran into the crowd, and rescued Paul. Because Lysias couldn't get a clear answer from the Jews why they tried to kill Paul, he put Paul in chains and took him to the barracks. There, he ordered a centurion to flog Paul to find out why the Jews wanted to kill him. Flogging a prisoner to learn the truth was standard practice in Roman times. As a centurion was about to order Paul flogged, Paul asked if it was legal to flog a Roman citizen who wasn't found guilty of a crime. Paul knew the answer was "No," and so did the centurion. Immediately, the centurion reported Paul's words to Commander Lysias. Lysias was alarmed when he learned that he put a Roman citizen in chains.

The following day, Lysias convened the Sanhedrin and took Paul into the assembly. For the most part, the Sanhedrin was composed of Sadducees and Pharisees. In contrast to Pharisees, Sadducees didn't believe in the resurrection of the dead. Paul was a Pharisee. When he declared that he was on trial because he believed in the resurrection, an argument ensued between the Pharisees and Sadducees. The two groups were so combative that Lysias removed Paul, fearing that Paul would be torn apart.

The next day, forty Jewish men vowed not to eat or drink until they killed Paul. Paul's nephew apprised Commander Lysias of the death threat. Lysias was determined to get Paul out of Jerusalem. He ordered two centurions with two hundred soldiers, seventy horsemen, and two hundred spearmen to leave during the night and take Paul to the safety of Governor Felix in Caesarea Maritima.

Pondering Relationships

Often the Bible represented Roman military officers as harsh and thoughtless. Commander Lysias's actions demonstrated a career military officer who tried to live with the rebellious and volatile Jews rather than cruelly suppress them. When confronted with a lethal mob outside the temple, many Roman commanders would have squashed the riot by knocking Jewish heads together. Instead, Lysias rescued Paul and investigated the cause of the disturbance. Even after Lysias knew Paul was a Roman citizen, he was open-minded enough to consider whether or not the Jews had just cause to want Paul dead. He didn't assume that Paul's Roman citizenship meant he was without blame; nor that citizens—notorious for insurgency—were automatically wrong.

Readers suspect that Commander Lysias would have preferred to free Paul with a warning to get out of Jerusalem; but, he learned that forty Jews conspired to kill Paul. Given Paul's Roman citizenship, Lysias couldn't allow anarchists to kill him.

When Commander Lysias sent Paul to Governor Felix, he sent a letter to the governor. He wrote that he rescued Paul because Paul was a Roman citizen. This part of the letter was a misrepresentation. Lysias's rescue was unrelated to Paul's citizenship. Demonstrating leadership, Commander Lysias didn't send Paul to Governor Felix without a follow-up plan to resolve the problem. He ordered Paul's accusers to present their case against Paul before Felix.

Just as Nebuzaradan saved Jeremiah's life, so Lysias save Paul's life. Our sense is that both commanders would meet John the Baptist's criteria for appropriate military behavior, i.e., soldiers shouldn't extort money or falsely accuse people.

Reflection

Which of Commander Lysias's behaviors do you want to display and avoid in your own relationships?

Julius, Upright Centurion
Acts 27; 28:1–16

Heart of the Story

Julius was the centurion who took Paul to Rome. Julius saved Paul's life during a destructive storm at sea.

Story Line

Because Paul appealed to Caesar, Governor Festus sent Paul to Rome. Julius, a centurion attached to the imperial Augustan Regiment, transported Paul and other prisoners from Caesarea Maritima to Rome. Julius, soldiers, and prisoners traveled on ships that depended on the wind to take them west across the Mediterranean Sea. They traveled in mid-to-late October. At that time, the Mediterranean Sea was swept by fierce storms. Eventually, their ship reached Fair Havens on the south-central coast of Crete. Fair Havens wasn't a good winter port. The ship's pilot and owner convinced Julius to sail for Phoenix, about forty miles west of Fair Havens.

Paul warned Julius not to leave Fair Havens; however, Julius disregarded his warning. Soon after leaving port, hurricane-force winds hit the ship and continued fourteen days. Cargo, ship's tackle, and furniture were thrown overboard. Anchors were dropped to slow the ship's speed. Sailors were so busy pumping water and trying to keep the ship from capsizing, they had no time to eat.

Eventually, the ship approached land. Now, the problem was that it could run aground and be battered apart by winds and crashing waves. The sailors understood the problem and attempted to escape, using a small boat kept on the ship. Paul told Julius that unless the sailors remained onboard the ship, neither soldiers nor passengers would live through the storm. Julius ordered his soldiers to cut the dinghy's ropes. It fell into the ocean and drifted from the main ship; thus, sailors had to remain onboard the vessel.

The next morning, the sailors saw land. Striking a crosscurrent, they ran aground on a sandbar. As anticipated, the ship began to break apart, buffeted by violent waves. The Roman soldiers wanted to kill all prisoners to prevent their escape; but, Julius stopped his men. He ordered soldiers and prisoners to swim ashore or hold onto boards and float to shore.

Despite the terrible storm and total destruction of the ship, not one of the 276 ship occupants was lost. They landed on Malta, where islanders provided for their needs. After three months, Julius obtained passage for his group on another ship. Eventually, they arrived in Puteoli, the chief port for Rome. A week later, they traveled overland to Rome.

In Rome, Julius delivered his prisoners to the guard captain. At that time, Sextus Afranius Burrus was the commander of the Praetorian Guards. He was fair in his treatment of prisoners. Commander Burrus had the final say about where Paul would be confined while he awaited trial in Nero's court. Festus's weak judicial case against Paul in combination with Centurion Julius's report of Paul's exemplary behavior during the trip, led Burrus to place Paul under house arrest, rather than imprison him.

Pondering Relationships

Luke, who wrote the book of Acts, accompanied Paul when Centurion Julius took him from Caesarea Maritima to Rome. In his narrative of the trip, Luke presented Julius as a confident, decisive officer, open to advice even from a prisoner. Julius cared for his men. He prevented sailors from abandoning the beleaguered ship, which would have resulted in its sinking. He refused to allow his soldiers to kill prisoners, knowing he risked death if any escaped. Readers don't know the source of Julius's integrity and ethics, but they guided his decision-making.

Similar to most New Testament centurions, Julius was capable. He followed military orders, but made prudent decisions for the humane treatment of his prisoners. Julius recognized that Paul had foreknowledge of the ship's fate. Perhaps, he believed Paul's strange tale that an angel told Paul no lives would be lost during the storm. Roman centurions saw many extraordinary events in their military experiences. Often, they were open-minded.

During the three month stay on Malta, Julius saw Paul's extraordinary healing powers. Even though Luke, a physician, traveled with Paul, Paul healed Publius's father and many other Maltese inhabitants. When the soldiers and prisoners arrived in Puteoli, Julius allowed Paul to spend a week with Christian brothers. Very likely, Julius assigned a soldier to guard Paul in Puteoli; nonetheless, Julius believed in Paul's integrity.

Reflection

Imagine what would have happened to Paul if Centurion Julius failed to stop the sailors from escaping the ship in the dingy, or if he allowed his soldiers to kill all prisoners. What do Christians owe to this Roman centurion?

Contemplation

General Colin Powell said, "The day the soldiers stop bringing you their problems is the day you stopped leading them. They have either lost confidence that you can help them or concluded that you do not care. Either case is a failure of leadership." Do you think General Powell was correct in his assessment of the need for military leaders to be accessable to their soldiers?

Pondering Military Officer Relationships

1. Ponder the four Old Testament criteria used to exempt an Israelite from military service. Would they work in the United States military? Would using the criteria enhance or depress morale in today's United States fighting force?

2. If you were a pagan Roman Empire officer, what would you have thought when assigned to Jerusalem, where Jews constantly fermented rebellion? Would you have tried to form a relationship with temple leaders and the populace, or simply used force to subdue them?

3. Currently, the United States military includes chaplains on the battlefield. Chaplains are for soldier's benefit, i.e., to provide the sacraments and offer them counsel and solace. Do you you think a chaplain's presence enhances or retards relationships between officers and enlisted men?

Chapter 10

Priests and Pastors

In ancient times, almost every nation worshipped gods and built temples dedicated to them, e.g., the Egyptians worshipped Ra, Moab worshipped Baal of Peor, and Zeus was the chief Greek god. Each temple had a cadre of priests. Priests made sacrifices to their god and interpreted their god's wants and actions to worshippers. Priests had two primary relationships: with their god and with worshippers.

Israelite priests were set apart from the community to make sacrifices to God and to worship God. They were men from the tribe of Levi and the family of Aaron. The process of anointing and consecrating Aaron and his sons was called "ordination" (Leviticus 8 NIV). Literally, ordination meant "you shall fill his hands." Israelite priests filled their hands with the role/tasks of the priesthood given to them by God through Mosaic law. Only priests possessed enough holiness to approach the most holy place in the sanctuary; and, then, only after they made sacrifices for their own sins.

Specific responsibilities of the priesthood were to:

- Oversee sacrifices and offerings to God, e.g., atonement, thanks, and grain.

- Bless people and events, e.g., first harvest of the year.

- Act as God's voice as when they used the Urim and Thummim.

- Interpret God's will as expressed in the Torah.

- Preside over ritual purification.

- Carry out administrative roles, e.g., collect tithes, temple maintenance, and blow the trumpet on festive occasions.

The Israelite priesthood was an authoritative institution. At times, the relationship between the civil and ecclesiastical (priesthood) government was adversarial. Priests established and deposed kings, promoted or obstructed adherence to God's laws, and influenced the morals of the nation. Some were men of great integrity. Others were frauds, apostate, and opportunists.

In the Old Testament, the priesthood was a symbol, or type, of Christ. Priests were coworkers with angels to prepare Israel for Christ, the ultimate high priest for the world. In the New Testament Christian church, Christ is the high priest. Sometimes, early Jewish converts continued to go to synagogues to worship. Gentile converts rarely attended synagogue or had contact with Jewish priests. In the budding Christian church, the close equivalent to the Jewish synagogue priest was the pastor.

In New Testament scriptures, the words *pastor, overseer,* and *elder* were used interchangeably. The pastor was the spiritual leader in a local church or congregation. Often, the pastor had authority by virtue of his experience and age (elder). He was an overseer in the sense that he supervised, inspected, and examined the beliefs of local church members. He officiated at church worship. Ability to teach was the distinguishing mark of a pastor in the new Christian church (Titus 1:9). Teaching included a sure knowledge of what was right and wrong (sound doctrine), ability to refute error, and courage to rebuke anyone who contradicted sound church doctrine. Paul's plan was for each town to have a church and a pastor.

In this chapter "Priests and Pastors," stories of five priests and one pastor are sequenced, from the most immoral and corrupt to the ideal, finest behavior. As you read through the stories of these clergy, compare and contrast their relationships with God and with their congregations:

1. Jonathan, sham priest
2. Uriah, apostate priest
3. Pashhur, chief of temple police
4. Jeshua, restoration priest
5. Titus, New Testament pastor
6. Azariah, courageous priest

Jonathan, Sham Priest
(Judges 17–18)

Heart of the Story

Jonathan was a fraud, opportunist, and thief. First, he agreed to be the priest for Micah's house. Later, he became priest for the Danite tribe.

Story Line

Although the story of Micah's priest is placed near the end of Judges, the events occurred two to three generations after the Israelites entered the Promised Land. The story is a glimpse of the low moral and religious life of early settlers.

Jonathan, a young Levite, left his home in Bethlehem, Judah, to seek a position. Bethlehem wasn't one of the forty-eight cities given to the Levites when Joshua administered the distribution of land in Canaan. Because Jonathan wasn't part of the Levite establishment, his needs weren't met by tithes and offerings. Jonathan needed a job. When he arrived at Micah's home in Ephraim, Jonathan found that Micah had two graven images in a shrine, along with household gods. Micah had ordained one of his sons to be priest for the various gods. The son wore an ephod, a vestment that was to be worn only by Israelite priests.

Micah offered Jonathan the position of priest in his home, with an annual salary of ten pieces of silver, plus food, housing, and clothes. Jonathan agreed, and Micah consecrated him as priest in his house. Micah treated Jonathan as a son. Micah believed that God would favor him because he had a Levite priest.

Later, six hundred Danite men and their families migrated north-ward from their tribal lands, south of Ephraim. They passed into the Ephraim hill country and came to Micah's house. As they stole the idols, household gods, and ephod from the house, Jonathan protested. The Danites proposed that Jonathan come with them. Persuasively, they argued that it was better for Jonathan to be priest for a tribe, than in a man's home. Jonathan agreed. He carried the idols, teraphim, and epod from Micah's house.

When the Danites arrived in Laish, in northern Canaan, they con-quered the local people. There, the Danites set up the graven images as their gods. Jonathan and descendants continued as priests for the Danite tribe.

Pondering Relationships

Jonathan was the son of Gershom, who was the son of Moses; thus, Jonathan was Moses's grandson. Importantly, he wasn't a descendant of Aaron. Although a Levite, Jonathan was ineligible to be an Israelite priest.

At this time in Israelite history, Shiloh was the center for worship of Yahweh (Joshua 18:1). The original Ark of Testimony and other taber-nacle furniture were located at Shaloh. At most, Shiloh was ten miles from Micah's home. Aaron's descendants were priests at Shiloh. Very likely, Jonathan stopped at Shiloh as he searched for a job.

It is tempting to conclude that Jonathan allowed himself to be made a priest because he didn't know any better. For some reason, he was raised in Bethlehem—not in one of the towns set aside for Levites. Possibly, Jonathan didn't know the Mosaic law that priests were to be Aaron's descendants. Perhaps, Jonathan believed all Levites could be priests.

Realistically, Jonathan knew exactly what he was doing. He didn't care about the distinctions between Levite and priest. In his egocentricity, Jonathan concluded that he would be a better priest than Micah's son. Whoever heard of an Ephraimite priest? Jonathan was more concerned about securing a good position, a comfortable income, and living with a wealthy family than obeying Mosaic laws for the priesthood.

Even if Jonathan didn't know God's requirements for the priesthood, he knew God's prohibitions against worshipping graven images. As he was growing up in his father's home, he heard the story of God's anger at Israel's worship of the golden calf in the wilderness. That Moses's grandson facilitated worship of idols and graven images exposes how quickly Israelites deserted God, after they entered the Promised Land.

When the Danites proposed that Jonathan become their tribal priest, Jonathan stole Micah's images, household gods, and ephod. He made no effort to stop the Danites from threatening Micah, the man who took him into his home and treated him as a son. Jonathan demonstrated no loyalty to his patron or to his God.

Reflection

It is difficult to find anything positive about Jonathan's relationship with God or with Micah. Ponder how Jonathan's moral compass allowed him to steal from Micah and practice idolatry.

Uriah, Apostate Priest
(2 Kings 16)

Heart of the Story

Uriah followed King Ahaz's directions to construct an Assyrian-style altar for the temple courtyard. Uriah was culpable in introducing foreign idol worship into God's temple.

Story Line

When the kings of Israel and Aram joined forces to wage war on Assyria, they asked Ahaz, king of Judah, to join them. Ahaz refused. Subsequently, the combined armies of Israel and Aram besieged Jerusalem. Frightened, King Ahaz turned to Assyria, rather than to God, for help. He took gold and silver from the temple and the palace treasury and sent them to Tiglath-Pileser III, king of Assyria. Ahaz implored

Tiglath-Pileser III to rescue Judah from Israel and Aram. He promised that if Assyria rescued Judah, the nation would become subject to Assyria.

Almost immediately, Tiglath-Pileser III marched against Damascus, Aram's capital. He captured the city and killed King Rezin. Then, he invaded Israel. Large areas of Israel came under Assyrian control. Captives from both Israel and Aram were carried into Assyria.

When King Ahaz went to Damascus to meet Judah's new overlord, Tiglath-Pileser III, he saw an altar. Ahaz sent an exact model of it to the Israelite priest Uriah and ordered Uriah to build it. Uriah was the only temple priest named under King Ahaz; probably he was chief priest.

Uriah had the Assyrian-styled altar built and in the temple courtyard when Ahaz returned to Jerusalem (720 BC). After viewing the altar, King Ahaz went up on it. There, he made burnt, grain, drink, and fellowship offerings. The writer of Second Kings didn't explicitly record if King Ahaz made the sacrifices to an Assyrian god or to God; however, Ahaz probably made the sacrifice to Assryia's god. Later in his reign, Ahaz worshipped and made sacrifices to foreign gods, to include offering his firstborn son to Assyrian gods (2 Chronicles 28:1–4).

Pondering Relationships

When Ahaz returned from Assyria to Jerusalem, Uriah didn't make the offerings on the new altar. King Ahaz made them. Heretofore, anything to do with the temple altar was the exclusive domain of the priests. Along with the new altar, Ahaz introduced new procedures in temple worship; kings now made offerings and sacrifices in the temple. There is no record that Uriah, or any temple priests, objected to Ahaz's actions.

At Ahaz's direction, Uriah moved the Bronze Altar from its central place in the temple courtyard and replaced it with the new Assyrian-styled altar. Going forward, the new altar was to be used for all offerings and sacrifices. The Bronze Altar was placed on the northside of the Assyrian-style altar. Ahaz planned to use the Bronze Altar for divination. On the Bronze Altar, Uriah would study entrails of sacrificed animals to determine the will and intentions of God! What a horrible way to descecrate the Bronze Altar.

The priest Uriah was guilty of apostasy. He abandoned and renounced loyalty to Mosaic law. What could Uriah have been thinking? Some possibilities are:

- Uriah was concerned with his own life and well-being. If he complied with Ahaz's direction, he would retain his life and position as chief priest. If he refused or protested the king's plan, he would be murdered or demoted.
- The new Assyrian-styled altar was bigger and more attractive than the Bronze Altar. Uriah concluded that the new altar added to the prestige of the temple and to his own prestige.
- An Assyrian-styled altar in God's temple demonstrated the temple was loyal to Tiglath-Pilneser III and Assyria. This outward loyalty could prevent more temple gold and silver being sent to Assyria.
- Uriah didn't believe in the art of reading entrails, therefore, justified his participation as meaningless.

During Uriah's tenure as chief priest, Jerusalem temple worship was superseded by officially sanctioned idolatry. On high hills and under green trees, people made sacrifices to various deities at upright stones and pillars.

Reflection

How did Uriah prioritize his relationships? Who was most important? Do you ever put your own life and well-being over your relationship with God? Ponder how and why you do this.

Pashhur, Chief of Temple Police
(Jeremiah 19:14–15, 20:1–18)

Heart of the Story

Priest and chief officer of the temple, Pashhur acted outside Mosaic law. He had Jeremiah beaten for prophesying God's words.

Story Line

God's prophet Jeremiah went to the temple courtyard. There, Jeremiah prophesied that God would bring disaster on Jerusalem because the people were stiff-necked and ignored God's words.

Pashhur was the head officer in the temple. Essentially, he was the temple chief of police. Pashhur maintained order and handled temple troublemakers. When Pashhur heard Jeremiah, he arrested him because Jeremiah's words were troubling and disruptive. Pashhur had Jeremiah beaten, then placed him in stocks. The stocks kept Jeremiah bent or stooped over at all times. They were located at the upper temple gate of Benjamin. Jeremiah's punishment and humiliation was visible to all who entered the temple.

Pashhur was present when Jeremiah was released from the stocks. Perhaps, Pashhur wanted to confirm that Jeremiah learned his lesson. Jeremiah wasn't intimidated by the beating or confinement. He looked at Pashhur and said that the Lord's name for him was no longer Pashhur but Magor-Missabib, which meant "terror on every side." Because Pashhur prophesied lies, God will make Pashhur a terror to himself and his friends. Pashhur will see his friends killed by the Babylonians. Judah and all the wealth of Jerusalem will be plundered and carried off to Babylon. Pashhur and his household will be carried into Babylon and die there.

Pondering Relationships

Jeremiah chapter 29 inaugurated a series of firsts into Jeremiah's life and message. Most came because of Pashhur's actions. For the first time, Jeremiah identified an enemy by name, i.e., Pashhur. Pashhur was the first of the prophet's enemies to confine or imprison Jeremiah. For the first time, Jeremiah's enemies inflicted physical violence on him. In his condemnation of Pashhur, Jeremiah named Babylon as Israel's enemy for the first time.

In later chapters, Jeremiah's enemies obtained the king's permission before persecuting Jeremiah; however, Pashhur didn't check his actions with anyone, not even the chief priest. Perhaps, Pashhur took his authority from the Mosaic law that said a guilty person should be flogged (Deuteronomy 25:1–3). If so, then Pashhur didn't follow the entire law. Mosaic law required that a person come to trial in court, where a judge decided guilt or innocence. The judge—not the temple chief officer—presided over the flogging. Further, Mosaic law made no provision for a guilty man to be placed in stocks after a flogging.

Jeremiah and Pashhur's adversarial relationship demonstrated the schism between God's word versus a synagogue hierarchy that catered to political power and influence. Likely, Pashhur believed his actions toward Jeremiah were the result of zeal for God's law, when he was actually pandering to King Zedekiah's corrupt, idolatrous reign.

Pashhur's actions mirror behaviors of priests and pastors in the twenty-first century who strive to be politically correct. What God has declared a sin in holy scriptures, man—even priests and pastors—cannot declare right.

Reflection

Summarize this priest's relationship with the prophet Jeremiah. Ideally, what would the priest-prophet relationship look like?

Jeshua, Restoration Priest
(Ezra 3:1–9, 5:1–2; Zechariah 3)

Heart of the Story

God replaced Jeshua's clothes, polluted by sin, with clean garments and demonstrated that God—not sacrifices, altars, or temples—forgives and justifies.

Story Line

When the Jews returned to Jerusalem from the Babylonian captivity, Jeshua (also known as Joshua) was the chief priest. He and Governor Zerubbabel were the Jewish leaders during the early restoration years. As soon as they arrived in Jerusalem, the restored exiles rebuilt the temple altar and began to make sacrifices on it (ca. 537 BC). Then, they started to lay the temple foundation. Jeshua, his sons, and brothers supervised temple builders.

Because non-Jews living in the area opposed temple construction, rebuilding slowed down (536–530 BC) and eventually ceased (530–520 BC). For about sixteen years, Jeshua and fellow priests offered sacrifices on the rebuilt altar; but, returned Jews spent most of their time building homes, cultivating crops, and nurturing livestock. During these years, harvests were poor. On August 29, 520 BC, God declared that harvests were poor because the Jews neglected to build his house. He stirred up the spirit of Jeshua, Zerubbabel, and the Jewish remnant so that within a month they resumed building God's temple.

About a month later, God gave the prophet Zechariah eight visions. The fourth vision focused on the chief priest, Jeshua. Jeshua stood in front of the angel of the Lord. Satan stood at Jeshua's right side and accused Jeshua of sin. Immediately, the angel said, "The Lord rebuke you, Satan" (Zechariah 3:2 NIV). The angel told Satan that the Lord chose Jerusalem; Jeshua was a burning stick that God snatched from the fire.

The angel ordered that Jeshua's filthy garments be replaced with rich, clean garments. The removal of Jeshua's dirty garments signified the removal of his sin and demonstrated that God had the power to justify, or make Jeshua clean. A clean turban was placed on Jeshua's head. The turban was a priestly mark of authority and signified direct access to God.

Pondering Relationships

The restoration was about one thousand years after God established the priesthood; yet, God still worked through priests. Initially, the priest Jeshua was dressed in filthy clothes. In scripture, often the condition of an individual's garments denoted their character. For example, soiled, filthy garments depicted sin while white or shiny garments spoke of being made sinless or cleansed. The pre-exile priesthood wasn't holy before God. Priests introduced foreign altars and idols into the temple and led Israel and Judah to worship idols. The new turban affirmed the priest's rightful access to God as the mediator between Jew and God.

After reclothing Joshua, the angel of God told Jeshua that if he would walk in God's ways, keep God's requirements, and govern God's house, then God would give Jeshua and priests a place among those standing in the presence of God. Standing in the presence of God meant that priests would have direct access to God.

Amazingly, the angel didn't stop with this awesome declaration. The angel told Jeshua that he and the priesthood were symbolic of things to come. God would send the branch, i.e., the Messiah, who will remove the sins of the land in a single day.

Reflection

How does the story of the priest Jeshua symbolize Christ? Explain how relationships among Jeshua, God, and the returned exiles mirror the relationships among Christ, God, and his church.

Titus, New Testament Pastor
(2 Corinthians 2:13, 12:18;
Galatians 2:1–3; Titus)

Heart of the Story

Titus was the quintessential New Testament pastor, who modeled obedience to God's word and submission to his mentor and bishop, Paul.

Story Line

Titus stands out as an early Christian pastor and Paul's fellow minister. Information on Titus is pieced together from various New Testament books and from early New Testament tradition. Titus was converted by Paul early in Paul's ministry. Possibly, they met when Paul and Barnabas preached in Antioch, or earlier when Paul ministered in Syria and Cilicia (ca. AD 37–47).

Titus was Greek. He accompanied Paul and Barnabas to Jerusalem to attend a church council meeting. In Jerusalem, the council acknowledged that Titus—and thus all Gentiles—didn't need to be circumcised to be members of the Christian church. By making this decision (decree), early church fathers moved Christianity from a sect of the Jewish faith (which required circumcision) to a separate religion. Christians didn't need to practice Judiasm.

Paul was concerned that the Corinthian church was divided because some of its powerful members were arrogant. Paul wanted members to drop their one-upmanship and work together to advance the good news of Christ, build up the faith in weak members, and effectively witness to unbelievers. Paul wrote the Corinthian church a "severe" letter admonishing them; however, Paul feared how the Corinthians would react negatively to his bluntness. Paul gave Titus the challenging task of delivering his letter to the Corinthian church (AD 53–55).

Between Paul's house arrest and his final imprisonment in Rome, Paul completed a fourth missionary journey where he, possibly, went to Spain and, most definitely, to Crete (ca. AD 62–64). Titus was with Paul in Crete. Paul's normal pattern when establishing new churches was to appoint church elders. For some reason, this pattern was not, or could not be, followed in Crete. Titus remained on the island when Paul left. His job was to bring order to the new congregations.

Paul wrote a letter to Titus in AD 63–64 from Nicopolis, a port city about two hundred miles northwest of Athens. He urged Titus to come to him in Nicopolis. Probably, Titus met Paul in Nicopolis, but didn't remain with Paul. In the last Bible account of Titus, he is busy establishing the Christian church among the aggressive Dalmatians.

Pondering Relationships

Titus did a masterful job of interpreting Paul's letter and Paul's concerns for the Corinthian church. Through Titus's efforts, church members responded by longing for Paul's presence, mourning over their sins, and with zeal for Paul's ministry. Titus's labor with the Corinthian church took longer than either Titus or Paul anticipated. Titus didn't join Paul at Troas as planned but joined him later in Macedonia.

Titus had an uphill battle as he worked to establish and pastor churches on Crete. Cretans were described as liars, evil beast, and lazy gluttons (Titus 1:12). Throughout the ancient world, Cretans were known for their immoral lives. Almost immediately, false teachers arose in the individual Cretan churches, i.e., some Jews advocated circumcision for Gentile converts, others obsessed on Jewish myths. Titus traveled among the infant churches to organize them, appoint elders, and refute false doctrine.

Reflection

Why do you think Titus was so obedient to Paul's instruction and wishes? Do you think Titus, being a Gentile (Greek) rather than a Jew, helped or hurt his pastoral work?

Azariah, Courageous Priest
(2 Chronicles 26:16–21)

Heart of the Story

Azariah, a courageous chief priest, confronted King Uzziah when the king attempted to burn incense in the temple.

Story Line

Azariah was the chief priest when King Uzziah (also known as Azariah) ruled Judah. Azariah means "Yahweh has helped" or "Yahweh is my helper." It was a common biblical name, particularly among priests.

Uzziah became king when he was sixteen years of age (792 bc). As long as Uzziah's mentor, the prophet Zechariah, lived, Uzziah sought the Lord and had great success. He won battles against the Philistines, Arabs, and Meunites. Uzziah completed several building projects, e.g., repaired the Jerusalem walls and built cisterns. He increased the security of Judah by establishing a large, well-trained, and well-equipped army. He hired engineers to install war machines on Jerusalem walls.

Eventually, Uzziah's strength made him proud. His pride led him to become unfaithful to God. The event that precipitated Uzziah's downfall occurred when Uzziah entered the temple sanctuary and prepared to burn incense on the Incense Altar. He had an incense censor in his hand when the chief priest, Azariah, and eighty courageous priests confronted him. Azariah reminded King Uzziah that only priests were consecrated to burn temple incense. Uzziah broke God's law by trespassing into the sanctuary. Azariah asserted that Uzziah's actions didn't honor God; he demanded that Uzziah leave the sanctuary. At this point, Uzziah still had the opportunity to repent and leave the sanctuary without incurring God's wrath.

Instead of submitting to Azariah's direction, Uzziah started to rage at him. Immediately, leprosy broke out on the king's forehead. When Azariah and the priests saw the leprosy, they hurried Uzziah out of the sanctuary and temple complex. Uzziah's leprosy persisted throughout the remainder of his life. Uzziah's son, Jotham, governed Judah. When Uzziah died, he wasn't buried in the kings' tombs because of his leprosy.

Pondering Relationships

Azariah was a strong chief priest who was unafraid to confront a powerful king, a king who was one of the most successful in Judah's history. Azariah knew the roles and responsibilities of the priests. As high priest, Azariah felt secure enough to lead other priests to confront King Uzziah's behavior.

Azariah understood God established a separation of church and state in Israel. As king, Uzziah had the right and responsibility to act as head of the civilian government of Judah; however, the chief priest was God's representative on earth. They functioned as head of the temple. Uzziah had no right to declare himself head of the religious government of Judah, which he did by attempting to burn incense on the Incense Altar.

The Bible didn't record how Uzziah realized leprosy appeared on his forehead. Perhaps, he felt a change in his skin, saw flakes of skin falling past his eyes, or saw the shocked expressions on Azariah's face. After Uzziah's leprosy appeared, Azariah prevented him from touching priests, temple furniture, or accessories. If these items were touched by anyone with leprosy, they had to be recleansed and repurified. In reality, Uzziah was eager to leave the temple. Possibly, Uzziah thought that the leprosy would disappear when he exited the temple.

The Bible contains no evidence that King Uzziah contacted Azariah to offer sin and guilt offerings for his actions. Given the integrity with which Azariah approached his position as chief priest, he would have made the offerings willingly. Conceivably, Azariah even reached out to his king to attempt to restore him to a right relationship with God. Instead of admitting that he needed God's forgiveness, King Uzziah lived with his leprosy the last ten years of his life.

Reflection

When King Uzziah entered the temple and started to burn incense, Azariah confronted him in a matter of minutes. Azariah didn't have to step back and carefully think about the optimal way to respond. How and why do you think Azariah was able to respond so rapidly?

Contemplation

Reverend Billy Graham said, "The test of a preacher is that his congregation goes away saying, not 'What a lovely sermon!' but 'I will do something.'" Reading about Azariah causes us to aver, "I will have the courage to act out my convictions." Titus makes us want to be ambassadors for Christ, to include taking on tasks equivalent of setting up churches among liars and cheats.

Pondering Priets/Ministers' Relationships

1. Read the criteria for a pastor in 1 Timothy 3:1–7. Do you agree with all of them? Are there any that you would like to add or delete? Why is it important that pastors meet these criteria if they are to have successful relationships with God and their congregation?

2. The priest Jeshua was a symbol of the high priest, the Messiah to come. How did the Messiah, the branch, remove the sins of the people of Israel in a single day?

3. How do church members deal with major ethical sins in pastors? How can these sins impact pastors' relationships with church members and with God? Are you able and willing to forgive a pastor's sins?

CHAPTER 11

Prophets and Prophetesses

Prophets are some of the most famous and most loved characters in the Bible. Jesus was a prophet. The greatest leader in Israelite history, Moses, was a prophet. So were Elijah, Jonah, and Miriam. In the Bible, a true prophet was called by God. God initiated the relationship. Prophets spoke the actual words of God without any modification or interpretation. The Israelites were to both listen to and obey prophets whom God raised up.

Often God revealed messages to prophets through visions. At other times, the Bible didn't elaborate how prophets received God's words. An exception to the vision/perception pattern was Moses. God spoke to Moses directly (Numbers 12:8). Most prophetic messages began with, "The word of the Lord."

At times, Israel valued its prophets, while at other times, it detested them. Some kings sought and obeyed the words of God's prophets. Other kings had prophets tortured, even murdered. God's true prophets weren't afraid to hold kings and civilian governments accountable for their behavior. Prophets even reprimanded apostate priests for idolatrous and immoral behavior.

God gave prophets the gift of foreknowledge. For that reason, early in the Old Testament, prophets were called seers. Discernment was needed when pondering prophecies because some had stipulations, e.g., Jonah told Nineveh that *unless* they repented in the next forty days, their city would be destroyed. Because Nineveh repented, God spared the city. Foreknowledge was a criterion that separated true from false prophets. If a prophet proclaimed words in God's name and they didn't come true, the Israelites shouldn't fear the prophet. Rather, they should put the pretender to death.

False prophets were plentiful in the Bible. At times false prophets won over God's prophets. The false prophet Zedekiah convinced Kings Jehoshaphat and Ahab that Micaiah's prophecy was wrong. Zedekiah slapped Micaiah's face!

Although most Bible prophets were men, some were women, e.g., Huldah. No differences existed between the call and functions of male and female prophets. Some, priests were also prophets, e.g., Ezekiel and Jeremiah; perhaps, they had an income from the temple. Other prophets earned their income from jobs or were given gifts for their foresight. For example, Amos tended sycamore fig trees. Saul's servant suggested that Saul give Samuel money in return for information about the family's lost donkeys.

Prophecy wasn't solely an Old Testament phenomenon. Prophets were identified throughout the New Testament church. Agabus prophesied both a famine in Jerusalem and Paul's imprisonment. Philip's four daughters were early church prophets. The author of Revelation, John, was a prophet. A gift from the Holy Spirit, prophecy was given to the Christian church to prepare God's people for service and to build the body of Christ into mature unity. Paul considered prophecy the most desirable spiritual gift.

At the same time, Christ, Paul, and the apostles constantly warned people to watch out for false prophets. Christ said false prophets were like ferocious wolves that acted like gentle sheep. His good news was that people could recognize false prophets by their fruit—words and actions.

In this chapter, both male and female obscure prophets are identified. Four characters are from the Old Testament and two from the New Testament. Taken together, these six individuals present a picture of prophets in ancient Israel and in the New Testament church. Some are true prophets/prophetesses while others are false.

- A tale of two prophets.
- Oded, stalwart prophet.
- Huldah, Judah's prophetess.
- Noadiah, questionable prophetess.

- Agabus, New Testament prophet.
- Jezebel, Thyatiran church prophetess.

A Tale of Two Prophets
(1 Kings 13)

Heart of the Story

The unnamed prophet spoke God's words but didn't completely obey God. The old prophet lied and seduced a true prophet from following God.

Story Line

Under Rehoboam's reign, the ten northern Israelite tribes rebelled and created their own nation called Israel and the Northern Kingdom. Jeroboam was the first king of Israel. Jeroboam saw people of the Northern Kingdom traveling to Jerusalem to worship God in the temple and to celebrate annual feasts. Fearing religion would draw Israelite loyalty back to Jerusalem and Judah, Jeroboam established two centers of worship in Israel. One was in the far north near Mount Herman in the tribal lands of Dan. The second was at Bethel, about twelve miles north of Jerusalem, close to the border between Ephraim and Benjamin.

At both centers, King Jeroboam set up golden calves and told the people, "It is too much for you to go up to Jerusalem. Here are your gods, O Israel, who brought you up out of Egypt" (1 Kings 12:28 NIV). Jeroboam appointed priests to make sacrifices to the golden calves. Many priests weren't Aaron's descendants. They were men who agreed to do the king's bidding.

One prophet who spoke against the Bethel shrine and altar wasn't named. In the NIV Study Bible, his story is titled, "The Man of God from Judah." The writer of Kings recorded that a prophet came from Judah to Bethel by the word of God. Exactly how God gave his message to the unnamed prophet wasn't recorded; however, God told the prophet three things: (a) take the message to Bethel, (b) don't eat bread or drink water in Israel, and (c) don't return from Israel the same way that you went there.

When the unnamed prophet arrived at Bethel, King Jeroboam was there. The king was on the altar, making sacrifices to the golden calf gods. The unnamed prophet cried out, "O altar, altar! This is what the Lord says: 'A son named Josiah will be born to the house of David. On you he will sacrifice the priests of the high places who now make offerings here, and human bones will be burned on you'" (1 Kings 13:2 NIV). The prophet declared that as a sign from God, the altar would be split apart and the ashes poured out.

King Jeroboam heard the unnamed prophet's words. He stretched out his hand toward the prophet and ordered his soldiers to seize him. Immediately, Jeroboam's hand shriveled so that he couldn't pull it back. The altar split apart and its ashes poured out, validating the prophet's declared sign from God.

King Jeroboam was devastated by the sight of his hand. He asked the unnamed prophet to intercede for him so God would restore his hand. After the prophet prayed that God would restore the king's hand, it was completely healed. As a thank you, King Jeroboam asked the prophet to come home with him to share a meal. Jeroboam wanted to give the prophet a gift. The prophet refused, repeating God's words that he eat or drink nothing in Israel. Then, the prophet left and began to travel home a different way from his going to Israel.

If the story ended at this point, the unnamed prophet would have successfully enacted God's commission. Unfortunately, there is a second part to the story.

An old prophet lived in Bethel. When he heard what the unnamed prophet from Judah did at the Bethel altar, he went after him. The old prophet found the unnamed prophet sitting under a tree. The old prophet asked the unnamed prophet to come home and eat with him. The unnamed prophet declined, repeating God's command that he could eat or drink nothing in Israel. The old prophet persisted, identifying himself as a prophet. He averred that God's word came to him via an angel and directed the old prophet to bring the unnamed prophet home. The old prophet lied to the unnamed prophet; however, the unnamed prophet believed him and went to his home near Bethel.

As the two men were eating, the word of God came to the old prophet. He cried out that the unnamed prophet defied the Lord, when he came back to Bethel and ate and drank. Consequently, the unnamed prophet's body wouldn't be buried in the tomb of his fathers. As the unnamed prophet returned home to Judah, a lion killed him. The old false prophet retrieved the unnamed prophet's body and laid it in his own tomb. He ordered his sons to place his body beside the unnamed prophet when he died.

Pondering Relationships

Notice, Jeroboam didn't order his own Bethel priests to pray to their gods to heal his hand. Rather, he asked the unknown prophet to intercede for him to God. Despite acknowledging God was superior to his own god, Jeroboam didn't remove the shrine at Bethel. Hundreds of years later after the Northern Kingdom fell, King Josiah of Judah destroyed the Bethel shrine site.

The unknown prophet was a true prophet of God. He did God's will by traveling to Bethel and prophesying against the false gods there. He did God's will when he refused to eat with King Jeroboam. His fault was being seduced by the lies of a false prophet. The question is why did the unnamed prophet accept the old prophet's invitation after having the strength to turn the king's invitation down?

Conceivably, the two prophets knew each other. The community of prophets was small in Judah and Israel. At one time, the old prophet may have even been a true prophet of God. He fell so far from righteous behavior that he willingly implicated God's name in a lie.

Another factor in the unnamed prophet's decision to go to the home of the old false prophet was comfort. The Bible doesn't say how far his home was from Bethel. Perhaps, he traveled a full day to get to Bethel, spent a day prophesying, and had another day's travel to reach his home. Clearly, he was tired. The false prophet found him sitting under a tree. Tired, hungry, and thirsty, the unnamed prophet took the path that led to his comfort while disregarding God's direct commandments to him.

The old prophet averred that God changed his mind and allowed the unnamed prophet to eat and drink in his home. Today, some Christian false prophets claim God changed his mind since Testament times. They think that words of New Testament church fathers are outdated in a multicultural society. Specifically, today's false prophets aver:

- The twenty-first century God is more loving and forgiving than the God of the Old Testament.
- Individuals who embrace other religions will go to heaven because the true God is so good.
- God gave his son for the sins of the world, therefore, we are all forgiven and no one will perish.

When I hear these assertions, I am reminded of the old prophet and various false prophets in the final days of Judah, e.g. Hananiah and Pashhur. They related dreams that came from their own minds rather than speaking God's words. They offered messages of false peace, claiming that the walls of Jerusalem wouldn't be breached because God was their fortress. Like the old prophet, twenty-first century false prophets distort the truth. In reality, God and his word do not change (Malachi 3:6).

Reflection

Despite his culpability in the unnamed prophet's death, the old prophet retrieved his body and buried him in his own tomb. He mourned the unnamed prophet. Are you appeased by the old prophet's restitution? What do you think of both prophets' actions and relationships?

Oded, Stalwart Prophet
(2 Chronicles 28:1–15)

Heart of the Story

God's prophet, Oded, objected to the Israelites enslaving two hundred thousand wives, sons, and daughters of Judah after Israel defeated Judah's army.

Story Line

During King Ahaz's sixteen-year reign (735–715 AD) over Judah, Kings Rezin of Aram and Pekah of Israel (Northern Kingdom) joined forces and attacked Judah. Although Jerusalem's walls weren't breached, Pekah killed 120,000 Judah soldiers, including some of the most significant men in Judah's army. Both Kings Rezin and Pekah took captives from Judah to their countries.

As Israel's army approached Samaria with two hundred thousand captives and much plunder, the prophet, Oded, met them. He declared to the Northern Kingdom (Israelite) army that:

- Their victory over Judah only occurred because God was angry with Judah.

- Their rage in slaughtering Judah's soldiers reached to heaven.

- They intended to make slaves of men and women captives from Judah.

Then, Oded asked a simple question, "But aren't you also guilty of sins against the Lord your God?" (2 Chronicles 28:10 NIV). Emphatically, Oded demand that the army send the captives back to Judah for fear that God's fierce anger would rest on the army and Israel. Several leaders from Ephraim also confronted the returning army. Their message was the same as Oded's.

The Israelite army responded to the prophet's and Ephraim leaders' warnings. They gave up their prisoners and plunder. From the plunder, Ephraim leaders clothed all captives who were naked. They gave the captives food, drink, and healing balm. They took them to Jericho and restored the captives to fellow countrymen.

Pondering Relationships

Although kings of Israel were worshipping man-made gods, some inhabitants continued to worship the true God. Oded was God's prophet, who lived in the Northern Kingdom of Israel. Oded called the prisoners Israel's "fellow countrymen," which suggested he viewed Israel and Judah as one nation (2 Chronicles 28:11).

Normally, when an Old Testament prophet spoke, he began the message with, "Thus says the Lord," putting his message in the context that God, not he, was speaking. Oded didn't use this format, or the chronicler omitted the words in his record. Most likely, the chronicler assumed readers knew that Oded spoke God's words.

Samaria was in tribal lands of Manasseh. The Israelite army passed through Ephraim to get to their capital city. Possisbly, Ephraimite leaders delivered their warning as the army and captives passed through Ephraim. On the other hand, the leaders could have been in Samaria and delivered their message after Oded delivered his. This sequence mirrors the unfolding of events in Second Chronicles. Being in Samaria explains how the Ephraimite leaders were available to take charge of the captives and get them to Jericho.

The value of two hundred thousand slaves and plunder may have been equivalent to millions of dollars. It is tempting to think that King Pekah's conscience was stimulated by Oded's words about enslaving fellow countrymen; thus, he freed them. More realistically, King Pekah feared God's displeasure and the power of Ephraim's leaders.

Every time I read this story, I wonder: would the Israelite army have given up their captives and plunder just on the word of God's prophet, Oded? Chronologically, the Bible passage suggested that the king and army responded more to Ephraim leaders than to God's prophet. Perhaps, Oded gave Ephraim's leaders courage to speak out.

Reflection

Oded is the only prophet who protested the enslavement of two hundred thousand captives from Judah. This story demonstrated that God can use a lone voice to stimulate a ruler, an army, and civilian leaders to do the right thing. Was there any time in your life that you were, or you could have been, a lone voice for God?

Huldah, Judah's Prophetess
(2 Kings 22:11–20; 2 Chronicles 34:22–28)

Heart of the Story

Huldah authenticated the Book of Law found in the temple and foretold the destruction of Jerusalem. She helped to bring about spiritual revival in Judah.

Story Line

Josiah became king (640–609 BC) when he was eight years old. He attempted to turn Judah from idolatry back to God worship. In the process of repairing the temple, the Book of Law was discovered. Most scholars believe that the Book of Law was Deuteronomy. By this point, Judah had abandoned God and was ignorant of the law. When the Book was read to Josiah, he was devastated. He believed that God's righteous anger would fall on Judah because the nation rejected God and turned to idols. King Josiah ordered his top officials to inquire of God what would happen to him, Judah, and Israel's remnant.

The officials, including the temple high priest, went to the prophetess Huldah. Her husband, Shallum, was the keeper of the temple wardrobe. Writers speculated that Shallum was Josiah's teacher/mentor when Josiah was a child. Huldah lived in the second district, an area incorporated into Jerusalem as part of Hezekiah's western expansion of Jerusalem. Some Bibles annotated that Huldah lived in a college, also called a house of doctrine. The name Huldah comes from *chôled* meaning a weasel, from the animal's rapid gliding motion (Strong, 2010).

Possibly, Huldah was a relative of Jeremiah. The king's delegation went to her rather than Jeremiah because they believed, or at least hoped, that she would give a softer or more favorable interpretation of God's pending wrath on Judah (Neiman, 2001). In reality, Jeremiah's words would have been the same as Huldah's. Prophets and prophetess declared God's exact words without interpretation.

After the king's delegation made their request, Huldah's response began with, "This is what the Lord, the God of Israel, says" (2 Kings 22:15 NIV). Huldah's words weren't encouraging. God planned to bring disaster on Jerusalem and its people—all the curses written in the Book of Law—because Judah rejected him and worshipped other gods. Because King Josiah's heart was responsive to the Book of Law and because Josiah humbled himself before God, God would wait to destroy Jerusalem until after Josiah died in peace.

Pondering Relationship

Huldah's primary relationship was with God. She spoke God's words without embellishment or fear. Initially, she identified King Josiah as "The man who sent you to me" (2 Chronicles 34:23 NIV). Although a king, Josiah had no status before God. Only later did Huldah refer to Josiah as the king of Judah when she learned that he humbled himself before God.

Some Bible commentators questioned if Huldah was a true proph-etess because King Josiah didn't die a peaceful death. He was killed in a battle with Pharaoh Neco. Importantly, Pharaoh Neco warned Josiah that God would destroy Josiah if he battled Neco. King Josiah ignored Pharaoh's warning; he was wounded in the battle between Egypt and Judah's armies. Josiah's officers took him back to Jerusalem where he died. Pharaoh Neco didn't follow the wounded king back to Jerusalem or besiege the city.

Josiah's death occurred because he disobeyed God's word given by the mouth of a pagan pharaoh. Probably, Josiah's own advisors warned him to avoid a battle with Egyptian forces. The way Josiah died doesn't negate Huldah's prophecy. Had Josiah not entered into battle with Neco, he could have lived longer than his thirty-nine to forty years.

Huldah's place of prophecy was between the first temple's two south-ern and busiest gates (Neiman, 2001). When the second temple was built, the gates were named after Huldah to commemorate her teachings and prophecy. Excavations on the second temple site revealed that the Huldah Gates were built directly on top of the area where Huldah sat. At the present time, the two gates of Huldah are blocked by stone in the Jerusalem old city.

Reflection

Like her namesake, the weasel that digs an intricate system of tunnels linking an entire community, Huldah linked the despair of the first temple's final days to the hopeful new generation of the second temple (Neiman, 2001). How would you describe Huldah's relationship with King Josiah?

Noadiah, Questionable Prophetess (Nehemiah 6:14)

Heart of the Story

Nehemiah prayed that God would remember Noadiah and other prophets, who gave him a bad name and discredited him.

Story Line

Noadiah lived in Jerusalem at the time Nehemiah was restoring the Jerusalem wall. Several aspects of Noadiah's life are controversial: First, was Noadiah a woman or a man? The KJV, NIV, and ESV identified Noadiah as a prophetess (Hebrew = *n'bîy'âh)*. In contrast, the Septuagint (translation of the Hebrew Bible into Greek) identified Noadiah as a man and used a masculine form for the word *prophet*. Possibly, the Septuagint was a mistranslation. The book of Ezra identified a man by the name of Noadiah.

The second question about Noadiah was her marital status. When women were named in the Bible, often they were defined in relation to their husband. Deborah was identified as the wife of Lippidoth, and Huldah's husband was Shallum. Noadiah was given no such designation. Possibly, she was never married, a widow, or married. Alternatively, her marital status was unimportant in Nehemiah's prayer.

The most significant controversy associated with Noadiah is whether or not she was a real or false prophetess. Nehemiah's prayer didn't suggest that Noadiah proclaimed false prophecies. In contrast, he named Noadiah a prophetess rather than a charlatan. Further, Noadiah seemed to be the most prominent of a cadre of Jerusalem prophets/prophetesses.

Pondering Relationships

The Bible doesn't provide information about Noadiah from her point of view. We know only the relationship that Nehemiah had with her. That relationship included that Noadiah both opposed and intimated Nehemiah. In ancient Israel, prophets often had an adversarial relationship with their kings and civilian governments, e.g., Isaiah and King Ahaz, Jeremiah and King Zedekiah. Nehemiah, who knew the history of Judah's prophets, shouldn't have been disconcerted by a prophetess opposing his policies.

The question becomes why and how did Noadiah intimate this credible leader? Why was he afraid of her and her cabal of prophets? The setting for Nehemiah's prayer is opposition to rebuilding the Jerusalem wall. As a Jerusalemite and woman, Noadiah knew the importance of a solid wall between herself and enemies. Likely, Noadiah wouldn't oppose rebuilding the wall. More likely, her opposition to Nehemiah was based on Nehemiah's focus on breaking apart families, in which Jewish men married non-Jewish women (Gafney, 2008).

The first group of Jews who returned from Babylon under Zerubbabel was mostly men. Over time, these men married pagan women and had children with them. Marrying women who weren't Jew was an act of infidelity for Israelites. When Ezra condemned these marriages, most men repudiated their non-Jewish wives. Children from the marriages were given into custody of their mothers. The divorced women and their children were left without status or identity—neither had a secure source of shelter or food. Despite their repentance under Ezra, Jewish men continued to marry non-Jewish women. When Nehemiah became leader of the restored Jews, like Ezra he vehemently condemned these mixed marriages.

Not unsurprisingly, Noadiah felt sympathy, even empathy, for these divorced women (Gafney, 2008). She was offended that Jewish fathers abandoned their children and allowed them to grow up without a father figure in the home. Her opposition could have been so strident and constant that it intimidated Nehemiah.

Reflection

Abandoning a wife who married in good faith and the children of the union seems harsh. The question is whether or not Noadiah's opposition—even intimidation—of Nehemiah on this point or another was from God or from her own feelings and beliefs.

Agabus, New Testament Prophet
(Acts 11:27–30, 21:10–12)

Heart of the Story

Agabus was a first-century Christian prophet. He was so well-regarded that knowledgeable hearers immediately accepted his prophetic words.

Story Line

Agabus was an elder in the Jerusalem church. In Acts, Luke recorded two incidents in which Agabus foretold events. Both occurred outside Jerusalem; the first in Antioch (modern Antakya) in the Roman province of Syria, and the second in Caesarea Maritima.

In the first incident, Barnabas and Paul were teaching in Antioch, where the largest Gentile church was located. Agabus and some other prophets traveled from Jerusalem to Antioch. Agabus stood up in a church assembly and predicted a severe famine, which would spread over the entire Roman Empire to include Jerusalem.

Despite the prophecy's future time frame, the assembled Christians in Antioch didn't doubt that Agabus's prophecy would happen. They determined to help the brothers in Jerusalem. Each gave according to his ability. Barnabas and Paul carried the gifts to the Jerusalem elders. Agabus's prophecy came true in the reign of Emperor Claudius (AD 41–54) when four famines occurred in the Roman Empire. Jerusalem was hit hardest in the second famine (AD 45–47).

The second time Luke recorded a prophecy from Agabus was about fifteen years later. By this time, Paul was the chief missionary in the Christian church. Agabus went to Paul and untied and took Paul's belt. Using the belt, Agabus bound his own hands and feet. There, Agabus said, "The Holy Spirit says, 'In this way the Jews of Jerusalem will bind the owner of this belt and will hand him over to the Gentiles'" (Acts 21:11 NIV).

Again, no one doubted Agabus's words. Instead they pleaded with Paul not to go to Jerusalem. Despite Agabus's dire warning, Paul traveled to Jerusalem. There, the Jews accosted Paul in the temple. Commander Claudius Lysias, the Roman tribune, rescued Paul from the Jewish mob. He sent Paul to Caesarea for trial in Governor Felix's Roman court.

Pondering Relationships

Agabus's Acts 11 prophecy of a famine in the Roman Empire was the first mention of the gift of prophecy in the early church. When Agabus gave the famine prophecy, Luke didn't record Agabus's exact words; however, Luke's record of Agabus's second prophecy began with the words, "The Holy Spirit says" (Acts 21:11 NIV). The New Testament church believed that prophecy was a gift from the Holy Spirit.

The Bible provides no additional information about this well-regarded New Testament prophet; however, Coptic Church tradition provides insight into Agabus's life and behavior (Coptic Orthodox Church Network, 2014). Agabus was one of the seventy-two disciples Christ selected to go before him to preach the gospel. He was in the upper room during Pentecost, where he received the Holy Spirit and the gift of prophecy.

Supposedly, Agabus died a martyr's death. Jerusalem Jews arrested and beat him severely. After putting a rope around his neck, they dragged him outside the city and stoned him to death. Catholic and Eastern Christian Churches consider Agabus a saint and dedicate feast days to him.

Reflection

How do you recognize a prophet today? What kind of relationships do prophets have? What would you *not* expect to see in a true prophet's relationships?

Jezebel, Thyatiran Church Prophetess
(Revelation 2:18–25)

Heart of the Story

Jezebel was a false prophetess in the Thyatrian church. Intentionally, she led other church members to sin.

Story Line

A small city, Thyatira was located in the fertile Lycus River valley of Asia Minor. Thyatira owed its importance to trade. Archeological evidence verified that Thyatira had guilds of woolworkers, linen workers, dyers, leatherworkers, tanners, potters, slave dealers, etc. The city's industrial base meant some women pursued careers outside the home, e.g., Thyatira was the home of Lydia, who sold purple cloth (Acts 16:14).

When Christ spoke to the seven churches of Asia Minor, his message to the Thyatiran church was the longest. Christ began by praising their love, faith, deeds, service, and perseverance. He noted that members were now doing more than they did at first; thus, they were growing spiritually. At the same time, Christ said that church members tolerated a woman he named Jezebel. Jezebel was a self-identified prophetess.

Some Thyatira church members sinned by eating food sacrificed to idols and by committing sexual immorality. Generally, church members were also guild members. Each guild had a patron gods or goddess. Before banquets, guild members sacrificed food used in the banquet to their guild idol. In first century Roman Empire, banquets devolved into sexual orgies.

Christ put the blame on Jezebel for idol worship and sexual immorality in church members. Her teachings led church members to these sins. Because Jezebel wouldn't repent, her outcome was dire. Christ said he would:

- Cast Jezebel on a bed of suffering.
- Make individuals who committed adultery suffer intensely, unless they repent of their ways.
- Kill Jezebel's children.

Pondering Relationships

The false prophetess, Jezebel, was the only person singled out for condemnation in Christ's message to the seven churches in Asia Minor. Probably, Jezebel wasn't the woman's actual name. Christ named her Jezebel because, like Old Testament Queen Jezebel, she taught and seduced others to practice idolatry and sexual immorality.

Possibly, casting Jezebel on a bed of suffering implied that she would become acutely ill and be bedridden. Alternatively, her suffering may have resulted from seeing followers suffer and die. In all probability, Christ wasn't referring to Jezebel's biological children but to individuals who followed Jezebel's teachings.

Jezebel abandoned God's word to search for the deep things of Satan. She promised followers secret spiritual knowledge. Her actions and promises alleged that followers could triumph over the satanic world while still participating in guild banquets. The key was not to believe in the false gods that food was sacrificed to.

Unlike a true prophetess, Jezebel's primary relationship wasn't with God. It may have even been with Satan, as she delved into dark spiritual secrets. Definitely, she put her relationship with followers over her relationship with Christ. Looking at Old Testament prophets, we see a different pattern of behavior. Hosea cared more about God than his wife. Jeremiah spoke God's message to the point where he was flogged and placed in stocks.

Reflection

How does seeing others sin lead to sin in ourselves or in our relationships? Do our actions lead others to sin?

Contemplation

The German satirist G. C. Lichtenberg (1742–1799) is purported to have said in his laconic style, "You can make a better living as a soothsayer than as a truthsayer" (Esar, 1968). Biblical false prophets seem to have lived more comfortably than many of God's true prophets. Certainly, some had more money and a greater following than God's true prophets. Mirroring the behavior of God's true prophets, we need to remember that earthly life is terminal; then, comes eternity.

The New Testament church is the body of Christian believers to include those in the twenty-first century. Prophecy can be important, even crucial, to believer's faith and spiritual growth.

Pondering Prophets' and Prophetesses' Relationships

1. Do people today, even individuals who identify themselves as Christians, believe that there are Christian prophets in the world? Where are the places to find present-day prophets (if they exist), i.e., Christian churches, seminaries, television, books, etc.?

2. Can an individual be a prophet/prophetess and articulate prophecies contrary to the Bible? How can we resist the teachings of false prophets? Have you ever had an "Aha" moment, when you realized that what you heard contradicted God's holy scriptures?

3. Hidden knowledge is seductive. Most of us like the idea of knowing what is hidden from others. That's one way Jezebel of Thyatira obtained her power. How can you resist a false prophet/prophetess who uses this technique?

CHAPTER 12

Magicians and Diviners

Magic and divination were highly developed and widely used in the ancient world to include by the Hebrews. Originally, magic was the science or art of the Persian priestly caste (magi). Like Levites, magi were devoted to religion. Over time, the word *magic* changed to mean occult (hidden, mysterious) rituals to control an outcome. Magic wasn't discerned with the eye or natural senses. It was supernatural and mediated by a practitioner. Often, magic was associated with use of trinkets, charms, and spells. At times, magicians mixed herbs to create spells.

Divination involved consulting beings or objects to gain information about the future or about subjects outside normal knowledge or thought. The Hebrew words for divination were translated witchcraft and soothsayer (Strong, 2010); however, in the Bible diviners had an assortment of names, e.g., sorcerer, witch, medium, spiritualist, spell caster.

Diviners used a range of techniques that included:

- Acting out a spirit entering and speaking through them.
- Interpreting dreams from a god, particularly when the petitioner slept in a sacred place.
- Reading omens, often from the entrails of animals, e.g., the liver.
- Describing the future using water, stars (astrology), or a divining rod.
- Throwing or drawing lots.

Throughout the Bible, God's people turned to mediums and spiritualists when they encountered fear and stress, and importantly, when they didn't get their own way. The Bible doesn't discount roles of magicians and diviners. Nor does it say that these practitioners were powerless. God took them seriously and talked about them from the Books of Law through Revelation. God's primary message was that he detested magicians and diviners because the origin of their behavior was from Satan (Deuteronomy 18:9–12).

Israelites were forbidden to use magicians and diviners for two reasons (Douglas and Tenney, 2011): First, use of magicians and diviners was denial of true prophecy and faith. Second, it was an attempt to make the future secure by knowing it in advance and avoiding its perils and pitfalls. Instead of trusting magicians and diviners, God wanted his people to recognize his sovereignty and trust him. God's question to occult seekers was, "When men tell you to consult mediums and spiritualists, who whisper and mutter, should not a people inquire of their God? Why consult the dead on behalf of the living" (Isaiah 8:19 NIV).

Moses told the Israelites that the practice of divination was the reason God would drive out the Canaanites when they entered the Promised Land. Christ grouped magicians with murderers, sexually immoral, and idolaters. He called them dogs. In New Testament times, dogs weren't the pet companions of today; they were dirty, mean, and vicious animals. Christ averred that the destiny of magicians is the fiery lake of burning sulfur.

In communities that were majority Christian, magicians and diviners were less common. In Ephesus, where Paul preached for over two years, individuals who practiced sorcery brought their scrolls together and burned them publically. When the total value of these scrolls was calculated, it was over fifty thousand drachmas. A drachma was a silver coin worth about a day's wage. The high value of the scrolls wasn't due to the price of the paper, but to the supposed power gained by secret spells outlined in them.

This final book chapter is about magicians and diviners. The late twentieth century showed a resurgence of interest in the occult, particularly in foretelling. As you read about these six Bible characters, draw comparisons between what happened in biblical times and what is occurring in your world.

- Jannes and Jambres, magicians
- Witch of Endor
- Women magician-prophetesses
- Bar-Jesus, Jewish sorcerer
- Simon Magus, the great one
- Philippian fortune-teller

Jannes and Jambres, Magicians
(Exodus 7:8–8:19; 2 Timothy 3:8–9)

Heart of the Story

Jannes and Jambres were Egyptian magicians. They were able to replicate several of Moses's miracles.

Story Line

God directed Moses and Aaron to meet with the Egyptian pharaoh and ask him to allow the Israelite slaves to go into the wilderness and sacrifice to God. In the first meeting, Pharaoh demanded a miracle to verify that Moses was speaking for his god and not for himself. Aaron threw his staff down. The staff turned into a snake. Pharaoh summoned the court sorcerers and magicians. Each magician threw down his staff. By occult arts, each staff became a snake; however, Aaron's snake swallowed the magicians' snakes. Despite Pharaoh seeing that Aaron's snake was more powerful than those of his sorcerer-magicians, he refused Moses's request.

Subsequently, God sent ten plagues on Egypt. In the first, the Nile River changed into blood, with the result that fish died. The second plague involved frogs leaving the river, ponds, and streams and emerging onto dry land. Pharaoh's sorcerer-magicians replicated both of these plagues by secret arts.

The third plague encompassed gnats. When Aaron struck the dust with his staff, gnats swarmed upon men and animals. The sorcerer-magicians weren't able to replicate this miracle. They told Pharaoh that the plague of gnats was the finger of God. Bible passages that described the subsequent seven plagues give no indication that Pharaoh demanded his magicians replicate them.

Pondering Relationships

Exodus didn't name the sorcerer-magicians who opposed Moses and Aaron. By Jewish tradition and in Paul's second letter to Timothy, their names were Jannes and Jambres. Paul claimed that they were men of a depraved mind, who opposed the truth. Their folly was clear to everyone.

Jannes and Jambres's powers were limited. Although they duplicated several of Aaron's actions, they couldn't undo them, i.e., stop frogs from swarming Egypt. Their inability to replicate Aaron's miracles of gnats made it clear that they couldn't elicit life from the dust of the earth.

Jannes and Jambres's relationship with Pharaoh depended on their success. When they couldn't produce gnats from dust, Pharaoh realized that their abilities were inferior to Moses's God. Pharoah dismissed the magicians from his court, demonstrating they had no durable relationship with him.

The two sorcerer-magicians had no relationship with the true God, the God of the Israelites. Yet, they had sufficient power to change a staff into a snake and the Nile River into blood. The Bible doesn't identify where Jannes and Jambres obtained their power, other than they had knowledge of secret arts. Most likely, their powerful actions originated from Satan. Egyptians believed in a pantheon of gods with Heka the ancient Egyptian god of magic. By praying to and worshipping Heka, Jannes and Jambres worshipped Satan, who acted on their behalf to oppose God.

Reflection

Both now and in the past, two supernatural powers operate in the world: God and Satan. With whom are you developing a relationship?

Witch of Endor
(1 Samuel 28)

Heart of the Story

The witch of Endor was a Canaanite woman, who contacted the dead Samuel for King Saul. When Saul became overwhelmed by Samuel's message, she cooked him a meal.

Story Line

The account of Saul and the witch of Endor occurred in 1010 BC, a day or two before King Saul's death. Endor was a Canaanite town that paid tribute to Manasseh. Earlier in his reign, Saul expelled mediums and spiritualists from Endor and the Promised Land. Likely, *expel* was a euphemism for killing them as Mosaic law required. By this point in Israelite history, Samuel was dead. No major prophet took his place.

King Saul's interaction with the witch of Endor occurred before a huge battle between the Israelite and Philistine armies. When Saul saw the size and might of the Philistine army, he was terrified. He asked God for help and direction. God was silent; he didn't respond to Saul's queries. In desperation, Saul asked attendants to find a medium, a woman who talked to spirits, so he could make inquiries about the pending battle.

A disguised Saul went to the witch of Endor's home. He asked the witch to bring up Samuel's spirit so Saul could consult him. Initially, the witch refused, saying Saul was setting a trap for her. In Israel, consulting the dead was outlawed. After Saul reassured her, the witch agreed to contact Samuel's spirit.

The witch brought up Samuel's spirit, but the spirit wasn't pleased with King Saul. Samuel told Saul that God turned away from him and gave his throne to David. The reason for God's action was Saul's disobedience. Saul didn't carry out God's judgment against the Amalekites. Samuel said that the Philistines would win the battle against the Israelites and Saul would be killed.

After hearing Samuel's ominous words, Saul collapsed. Now, the witch was really terrified! Immediately, she reminded Saul (and his men) that he promised not to kill her if she obeyed. When the witch learned that Saul was fasting, she offered to prepare a meal. Urged by his men, Saul agreed to eat. The witch killed and butchered a calf and made bread. After eating, Saul and his men left her home.

Pondering Relationships

The witch of Endor didn't worship the Israelite's God. Nonetheless, God used her to convey a clear message to King Saul—tomorrow Saul would die in battle.

Throughout this story, we detect that the witch doesn't trust King Saul and his men. Likely, she recognized that her visitors were Israelites. Initially, she denied any ability to contact spirits. She knew the Israelite law on witchcraft. She knew about the death or expulsion of many of her colleagues under Saul's reign. Likely, Saul's promise not to harm her, coupled with the offer of a rich payment, persuaded her to contact Samuel's spirit.

From the witch's point of view, the result couldn't have been worse. True, she contacted Samuel; but Samuel had a message of defeat and death for Saul. It was common for kings to kill the messenger who brought them bad news. Possibly, the witch's offer to make Saul a meal stemmed from self-preservation; however, the first-century Jewish historian Josephus wrote that compassion for Saul caused the witch to kill and cook her fatted calf (Whiston, 1987).

Conceivably, the witch of Endor was a fraud and swindler and had no real power. Maybe she was in league with Satan and worshipped demons. Yet, she didn't offer Saul platitudes i.e., everything will be alright or you will achieve a mighty victory over the Philistines. Instead, she spoke a message from God.

Reflection

Does God use individuals dedicated to Satan to do his will?

Women Magician-Prophetesses
(Ezekiel 13:17–23)

Heart of the Story

Some false prophetesses in Ezekiel's day were magicians. Deluded Israelites bought charms and veils from them to secure a safe future.

Story Line

Ezekiel chapter 13 is God's words through Ezekiel to false prophets, including false women prophets who used magic. Possibly, these women associated with each other in a guild-like arrangement. The prophetesses sold their magic charms and veils for insignificant sums because there were so many of them available for sale.

God accused false prophetesses of ensnaring souls of Israelites by having them tie magic charms around their wrists and wear magic veils. Because Israelites believed the prophetesses' lies, some were killed who shouldn't have died. Others, who should have died, were spared. These magician-prophetesses disheartened the righteous with their lies. They encouraged the wicked not to turn from their evil ways so their lives would be saved.

God asked the false women prophetesses if they thought they could trap others in magic without bringing destruction on themselves. God warned that he was going to tear the wrist charms and veils off individuals they ensnared. Once freed, the people wouldn't again fall prey to magic power. Finally, God told the magician-prophetesses that no longer would they see false visions or practice divination.

Pondering Relationships

In the Books of Law, God told the Israelites to write his laws on the doorframes of their home and gates, to wear them as symbols on their hands, and bind them on their foreheads (Exodus 13:9; Deuteronomy 6:6–9). Throughout history, some Jews took these verses literally. They tied phylacteries to their foreheads and left arm to remind them to remain faithful to God. Likely, the women magicians used this Mosaic commandment to seduce clients to wear charms on their wrists and to veil their foreheads.

When the Bible identified use of black arts, normally descriptive writers gave little or no information on magician/diviner's spells. The lack of specifics was deliberate. God wanted future magicians/diviners to have no resource or information to use as the basis for their own spells.

An Israelite's primary relationship was to be with God. Most assuredly, true prophet/prophetesses had to stay close to God in order to ascertain what God wanted him or her to say. These magician-prophetesses didn't do that. They profaned the name of God by claiming they received visions from him, when they didn't. Their visions were either a product of their own imaginations or given by a dark power. Their primary relationship was with Satan or one of his minions.

Have you ever wondered about these women's motivation? Were they deliberate charlatans, or did they believe their own actions? Did they trust what they read in tarot-like cards and/or the way stars aligned? When they went through a ritual to spell a charm, did they then believe that the charm had the ability to influence an outcome? Alternatively, were they driven to get ahead in the world? Was magic a means to provide financially for themselves and children? Whatever the reason for their behavior, the women lied to unsuspecting victims.

Reflection

Last Saturday, I participated in a church fair. Beside me, a woman sold beaded jewelry, e.g., amethyst, hematite. She claimed beads had power to influence a person's day. She said that each morning, she assessed how she felt. Then, she selected bead-constructed jewelry to enhance or negate her feelings. As a door prize, I won one of her bracelets. Should I wear it? Was she a type of magician or diviner?

Bar-Jesus, Jewish Sorcerer
(Acts 13:6–12)

Heart of the Story

The magician Bar-Jesus tried to keep proconsul Sergius Paulus from hearing the good news of Christ. Because of Bar-Jesus's opposition, Paul caused him to be temporarily blind.

Story Line

Barnabas and Paul's meeting with the sorcerer–magician Bar-Jesus occurred early in Paul's first missionary journey (AD 46–47). At the direction of the Holy Spirit, Barnabas and Paul left Antioch with young John Mark. The first country they went to was Cyprus, the home of Barnabas. They ministered across the entire island, finally arriving at Paphos, seat of the Roman government.

Sergius Paulus was the Roman administrator on Cyprus. He summoned Barnabas and Paul because he wanted to hear the word of God. Sergius Paulus was an intelligent man. An attendant of Sergius Paulus, Bar-Jesus, was a sorcerer-magician. He was referred to as Elymas, which meant magician or wizard.

Bar-Jesus opposed Barnabas and Paul's teaching. He attempted to dissuade Sergius Paulus from faith in Jesus Christ as savior of the world. Filled with the Holy Spirit, Paul looked directly at Bar-Jesus and called him a child of the devil, enemy of everything that is right, and full of all kinds of deceit and trickery. Then, Paul asked Bar-Jesus, "Will you never stop perverting the right ways of the Lord?" (Acts 13:10 NIV).

What followed was the first recorded miracle completed by Paul. Paul told Bar-Jesus that he would be blind, unable to see even the sun for a time. Immediately, mist and darkness came over Bar-Jesus. He groped about, seeking someone to lead him by the hand.

Sergius Paulus was amazed at the apostles' teachings about Christ. He marveled at what he saw them do. He became a believer in Jesus Christ as God and redeemer.

Pondering Relationships

At the beginning of this story, Bar-Jesus had a close relationship with Sergius Paulus. Bar-Jesus was with Sergius Paulus when Barnabas and Paul were summoned and began to explain the good news of Christ. Something about the story of Christ—son of God and redeemer of the world—alarmed Bar-Jesus. He began to oppose the apostles' teachings.

We aren't sure which part of the gospel Bar-Jesus attacked. It may have been that there was one God rather than the broad pantheon of Roman gods. Or perhaps, the opposition point was that God's son, Christ, was the only mediator between God and man. The intelligent Sergius Paulus would have deduced that if there was one mediator between God and man, he could, even should, pray directly to Christ. Wizards and magicians with spells and incantations were superfluous.

Whatever the exact focus of Bar-Jesus's opposition, his words caused Paul to conclude that he was "a child of the devil." What an indictment. Bar-Jesus's magic and sorcery were powered by Satan! His allegiance was to Satan, not to the proconsul.

If Paul ended his confrontation with Bar-Jesus only with words, Sergius Paulus would have concluded that two of the many Roman gods had a difference of opinion. Their earthly representatives had a simple, but heated, argument about who was the greater. What happened next cemented the apostles' arguments that Christ was the son of God, part of the Trinity. At Paul's words, Bar-Jesus became blind for a time. Probably, God chose to strike Bar-Jesus with blindness because Bar-Jesus tried to keep the proconsul in spiritual darkness.

Reflection

The Bible gave no indication that Bar-Jesus learned from this encounter. Even though he had an actual physical experience with God, he remained a child of Satan. Why would Bar-Jesus ignore such powerful empirical evidence?

Simon Magus, the Great One
(Acts 8:4–25)

Heart of the Story

Simon Magus the sorcerer wanted to increase his magic abilities. He wanted power to lay hands on people and fill them with the Holy Spirit.

Story Line

When the first major persecution of the new Christian church occurred in Jerusalem, many Christians left Jerusalem and the province of Judea. The scattered believers preached the gospel wherever they went. Philip, the evangelist, went to Samaria where he expelled evil spirits from individuals and healed paralytics and cripples.

Simon Magnus practiced sorcery in Samaria. He boasted that he was someone great. Some Samaritans said that Simon was the Great Power, referring to Simon as God himself. People gave Simon their attention and followed him because his magic amazed them. When Philip proclaimed the good news of Christ and healed individuals, many Samaritans believed in Christ. Simon was astonished by the great signs and miracles that Philip performed.

The apostles in Jerusalem heard that many Samaritans accepted Christ as their savior and were baptized; however, the newly baptized didn't receive the Holy Spirit. Jerusalem leaders sent Peter and John to Samaria. Peter and John laid their hands on new believers, and the believers received the Holy Spirit. Luke didn't record how the Holy Spirit manifested in the Samaritans. Most likely, it was the same way that Jerusalem believers evidenced the Holy Spirit on Pentecost, i.e., through a flame of fire over their head and the ability to speak in foreign languages.

Simon offered Peter and John money to tell him how they were able to lay hands on believers and transfer the Holy Spirit to them. Offended by Simon's belief that he could buy the gift of God, Peter said to Simon, "May your money perish with you" (Acts 8:20 NIV). Peter went on to tell Simon that because his heart wasn't right with God, Simon could have no part or share in Christ's ministry. Peter urged Simon to repent so God would forgive him for thinking he could buy the ability to give the Holy

Spirit to people. Insightfully, Peter told Simon Magus that he was full of bitterness and captive to sin. Hearing Peter's words, Simon pleaded with Peter to pray that nothing Peter said would happen to him.

Pondering Relationships

Simon Magus had a high level of self-esteem and confidence in his own abilities. He called himself, and allowed others to call him, the Great Power. In reality, he was a charlatan, a fake, who knew how to perform magic. Probably, he worked through illusions or was in league with Satan, who gave him power.

To get on Philip's good side and inner circle, Simon Magnus declared himself a convert to Christianity. Likely, he was even baptized. Simon followed Philip everywhere. He watched Philip closely to see if he could learn Philip's secrets. Were the cripples really healed by Philip, or did Philip plant them in crowds to demonstrate miraculous healing? Did Philip give these crippled individuals a secret drink, so that they could walk temporarily?

Conceivably, Simon Magus didn't believe his own magical abilities. Similar to his use of illusions and ploys to perform miraculous acts, Simon concluded that Philip used them. Further, who in the world was this Jesus who Philip kept talking about? Not for a minute did Simon think that a man the Roman's crucified came back to life. Say what you will about the Romans, they knew how to kill a man.

The problem was that Simon couldn't figure out how Philip performed the miracles. To make matters worse, two other men from Philip's magic guild came to town: Peter and John. These two were part of Jesus's inner circle. They had even more power than Philip.

When Simon asked Peter and John if he could buy the spell of laying on hands, his actions were congruent with the culture of magicians and sorcerers. They guarded their spells jealously. They shared them with other practitioners only when they were well paid. The more powerful the spell, the more it cost, i.e., a spell for raising the dead was more costly than a love potion.

After Peter's denunciation of Simon Magnus, Simon asked Peter to pray for him. For all the times Simon heard Philip teach, he didn't internalize that Christ, the redeemer of mankind, delights to forgive sins.

Simon didn't grasp that baptized believers had a personal relationship with Christ. If the Holy Spirit lived in him, Simon could pray for himself and have God hear him immediately. Perhaps, Simon Magnus didn't really believe in Christ despite his baptism.

Reflection

Church tradition teaches that Simon Magus was the first heretic in the Bible. From him, we get the modern word *simony*, which means making a business out of that which is sacred (MacDonald, 1995). Do you know self-identified Christians who make a business out of what is sacred? Think of some examples.

Philippian Fortune-teller
(Acts 16:16–38)

Heart of the Story

A demon-possessed slave girl identified that Paul and companions were God's servants. Paul demanded the demon leave the girl.

Story Line

Paul had a vision of a man telling him to go to Macedonia and help the people there. At once Paul, Silas, Timothy, and Luke traveled to Macedonia and overland to Philippi. A leading city in Macedonia, Philippi was a Roman colony. It was independent of provincial administration and had a government organized after that of Rome. Few Jews lived in Philippi; there was no synagogue. The Jews who lived in Philippi often met for prayer along the banks of the Gangites River.

As Paul and companions went to the river to pray, they met a slave girl. The girl had a spirit of divination. A demonic spirit lived in her and gave the girl information about the secret lives of people. She earned her owners a lot of money by foretelling.

The girl followed Paul and his companions, shouting, "These men are servants of the Most High God, who are telling you the way to be saved" (Acts 16:17 NIV). She kept this up for many days. Finally, Paul became exasperated with her harassment. He said to the demonic spirit, "In the name of Jesus Christ I command you to come out of her!" (Acts 16:18 NIV). Immediately, the demon left the girl.

When the girl's owners realized they could no longer make money through the girl's fortune-telling, they seized Paul and Silas. The owners took Paul and Silas before the Philippian magistrates. They accused the missionaries of teaching unlawful customs and creating an uproar in the city. The result was that Paul and Silas were severely beaten and spent the night in prison.

Pondering Relationships

Luke, who recorded this incident, identified the fortune-teller as a girl. This means that she was younger than the marriageable age of twelve to thirteen years. Possibly, she was eight to ten years old. We have no information on whether she was born or sold into slavery. Likely, she was a Macedonian Greek.

Although the Jewish culture forbids fortune-telling, the Greek and Roman cultures did not. In fact, Greeks valued the girl's ability. Greeks believed the slave girl possessed a pythoness spirit. The python was a mystical snake, worshipped as the Delphi oracle. For money, a priestess at Delphi answered petitioners' questions. The Delphi oracle focused on large national issues, i.e., where to build a colony or who would win a battle. Individuals—mostly girls or women—with a python spirit focused on foretelling secrets in individual lives, i.e., who would get a job, win a race, or marry.

The slave girl's owners gave her some freedom to move about Philippi. After she met Paul and his companions, she followed them. Luke gave no indication that her actions were hateful or mocking; however, she distracted the missionaries who were trying to teach the Philippians about Christ.

Likely, the girl's owners wanted—even expected—the missionaries to pay money to stop the girl from being a nuisance. Unfortunately, their expectation wasn't realized. Instead, Paul expelled the demon from the girl. She was left without foretelling power.

Have you ever wondered about the girl's reaction to the demon no longer living in her body? Maybe she felt relief. On the other hand, she could have felt alone, even empty, especially if the demon lived inside her since she was an infant or toddler. The girl had no idea how to live without the demon's presence. She may have worried how her owners would treat her now that her foretelling ability was gone. Would they punish her for following the apostles and losing her ability? Would they see her as useless? Would she be just another young female slave, worth little in a slave market? Probably, she had few, if any, friends in her owner's household. Other slaves/servants felt uncomfortable around her. No one would speak up for her.

The Bible recorded that Paul and companions left Philippi soon after being released from prison. Apparently, they had no further interaction with the slave girl, the demon who possessed her, or the girl's owners.

Reflection

How did Paul change the young slave girl's life by expelling the demon from her? Do you think that Paul had any responsibility for the girl after expelling the demon from her body? Would you have felt any responsibility for the girl if you were the source of such a major change in her life?

Contemplation

Diviners and magicians have power today. Their power source remains unchanged; it was and is Satan. For that reason, Christians need to avoid occult practitioners. When you read the six accounts, did you vacillate between who was the sadder, the magic practitioner or the individuals who contacted them? Despite any tug at emotions, Christians need to remember God's rule about contacting magicians and diviners.

Pondering Magician/Diviner's Relationships

1. Are you going to change any of your behaviors as the result of God asking you, "Should not a people inquire of their God? Why consult the dead on behalf of the living?" (Isaiah 8:19 NIV).

2. An American saying is, "Religion gives faith, the church gives hope, but nothing deceives like a horoscope." Have you ever had

your fortune told? Do you read your horoscope daily? If so, think deeply about the reason for these actions. Why do you do them?

3. If you saw that one god or entity was clearly superior to another, would you believe in the stronger god? In several of these six Bible accounts of magicians and diviners, God was clearly stronger than other gods. Yet viewers, e.g., Pharaoh, Simon Magus, didn't accept God. Why would anyone choose to worship a less powerful god?

References

Adeyemo, Tokunboh, ed. *Africa Bible Commentary*. Grand Rapids, MI: Zondervan, 2006.

Coptic Orthodox Church Network. "The Martyrdom of St. Agabus, One of the Seventy Disciples," 2014. http://www.copticchurch.net/.

Douglas, J. D., and Merrill C. Tenney. *Zondervan Illustrated Bible Dictionary*. Grand Rapids, MI: Zondervan, 2011.

Esar, Evan. *20,000 Quips & Quotes*. New York, NY: Barnes and Noble Books, 1968.

Gafney, Wilda C. *Daughters of Miriam, Women Prophets in Ancient Israel*. Minneapolis, MN: Fortress Press, 2008.

Walking Free Foundation. "Global Slavery Index 2014," 2014. http://www.walkfreefoundation.org/.

"Billy Graham Quotations." Accessed December 4, 2014. http://www.preach-the-gospel.com/Billy-Graham-Quotes.htm.

Hareuveni, Nogah. *Tree and Shrub in our Biblical Heritage*. Kiryat Ono, Israel: Neot Kedumim Ltd., 1989.

Hill, Andrew E. "A Jonadab Connection to the Absalom Conspiracy." *Journal of the Evangelical Theological Society* 30, no. 4 (1987): 387–390.

Hoshbach, Barbara. *Fools, Liars, Cheaters and Other Bible Heroes*. Cincinnati, OH: Franciscan Media, 1989.

Leman, Kevin. *What a Difference a Mom Makes, the Indelible Imprint a Mom Leaves on her Son's Life*. Grand Rapids, Michigan: Revell, 2012.

Lester, Meera. Woman of the Bible. Accessed November 16, 1014. http://www.net-places.com/woman-of-the-Bible/.

MacDonald, William. *Believer's Bible Commentary*. Edited by Art Farstad, Nashville, TN: Thomas Nelson, 1995.

Metzger, Bruce M., and Michael David Coogan, ed. *The Oxford Companion to the Bible*. Oxford, United Kingdom: Oxford University Press, 1993.

Neiman, Rachel. 2001. *The Prophetess Hulda, Her Message of Hope*. Accessed February 6, 2015. www.torah.org/learning/women/class51/html.

Powell, Colin. n.d. Colin Powell Quotes. Accessed on October 28, 2014. www.goodreads.com/quotes.

Rainey, Anson Frank. "The Satrapy 'Beyond the River.'" *Australian Journal of Biblical Archeology* 1, no. 2 (1969): 51–78.

Strong, James. *The New Strong's Exhaustive Concordance of the Bible*. Nashville, TN: Thomas Nelson, 2010.

The Works of Josephus, Complete and Unabridged. Translated by William Whiston. Peabody, MA: Hendrickson, Publishers, Inc., 1987.

Appendix

Little Known Bible Characters by Chapters

Chapter	Chapter Title	Characters
1	Husbands and Wives	Manoah and Wife, optimal marriage
		Amram and Jochebed, famous unknown couple
		Aquila and Priscilla, early church couple
		Elkanah and Peninnah, polygamous marriage
		Zimri and Cozbi, doomed marriage
		Hosea and Gomer, unloved marriage
2	Fathers and Daughters	Jairus's young daughter
		Acsah, beloved daughter of Caleb
		Daughters of Zelophehad, a deceased father
		Jephthah's sacrificed daughter
		Dinah and Tamar, daughters of unfaithful fathers (Jacob and David)

		Lot, father of immoral daughters
3	Mothers and Sons	Mother's advice to King Lemuel
		Lois, Eunice, and Timothy
		Zipporah and sons (Gershom and Eliezer)
		Shunammite woman's son
		Queen's Ano's dying son (Abijah)
		Murder of Rizpah's sons (Armoni and Mephibosheth)
4	Clans and Towns	The Gibeonites
		The Kenites
		The Recabites
		Elders of Succoth
		Men of Jabesh Gilead
		New Testament Lystrans
5	Masters and Slaves/ Servants	Naaman's valued slaves/ servants
		Hegai, eunuch over the harem
		Rhoda, excitable servant
		Onesimus, slave and son
		Bilhah and Zilpah, slaves or servants?
		Gehazi, greedy servant
6	Friends	Hushai, King David's friend
		Ebed-Melech, Jeremiah's rescuer
		Tychicus, Paul's friend and companion

		Job's friends (Eliphaz, Bildad, and Zophar)
		Hirah, friend of Judah
		Jonadab, Amnon's shrewd friend
7	Kings and Rulers	King Abimelech, Gideon's son
		Ish-Bosheth, shameful king
		Athaliah, woman ruler of Judah
		Hoshea, last king of Israel
		Jehoiachin, captive king
		Herod Agrippa I, proclaimed a god
8	Governors	Gedaliah, Nebuchadnezzar governor
		Zerubbabel, restoration governor
		Tattenai, impartial governor
		Rehum, manipulative governor
		Felix, inexperienced governor
		Festus, unscrupulous governor
9	Military Officers	Barak, reluctant commander
		Ittai, loyal Philistine commander
		Nebuzaradan, career Babylonian commander
		Johanan, fearful captain
		Claudius Lysias, Roman commander

		Julius, upright centurion
10	Priests and Ministers	Jonathan, sham priest
		Uriah, apostate priest
		Pashhur, chief of temple police
		Jeshua, restoration priest
		Titus, New Testament pastor
		Azariah, courageous Priest
11	Prophets and Prophet-esses	A tale of two prophets ("unknown" and "old")
		Oded, stalwart prophet
		Huldah, Judah's prophetess
		Noadiah, questionable prophetess
		Agabus, New Testament prophet
		Jezebel, Thyatiran church prophetess
12	Sorcerers and Magi-cians	Jannes and Jambres, magi-cians
		Witch of Endor
		Women magician-proph-etesses
		Bar-Jesus, Jewish sorcerer
		Simon Magus, the Great Power
		Philippian fortune-teller